About This Book

Why is this topic important?

When virtual classrooms were first introduced, much of the delivered content was in the form of lectures, and participant interaction was minimized. We simply did not know how to take full advantage of the medium. Now that virtual classrooms have become an expected addition to many e-learning programs, organizations are becoming more interested in making their live events more participant-centered and interactive.

One of the most common mistakes made when designing exercises for the virtual classroom is to try to re-create the interactions that were used in more traditional settings. Unfortunately, these exercises are not always effective. The live, online classroom is a new delivery medium with a variety of new collaboration tools, and we need to take advantage of these tools when designing in order to maximize our online events.

What can you achieve with this book?

Live and Online! Tips, Techniques, and Ready-to-Use Activities for the Virtual Classroom explores the process and critical concepts involved in designing effective online activities. It answers questions such as:

- How should instructional design be applied?
- How is my role as a designer impacted?
- What does online collaboration really mean?
- What are the critical success factors for creating effective learning environments for our participants?
- How do I design exercises for the collaborative tools available in the virtual classroom?

This book will assist instructional designers in creating programs that truly engage the audience and create effective and positively memorable learning experiences. Real examples and templates for the major tools can be adapted for use in your organizations, allowing you to create true online collaboration and elevate the impact of your virtual events.

How is this book organized?

The first three chapters of this book are focused on instructional design, creating effective learning environments, and online collaboration. Chapters 4 through 8 are concerned with specific collaboration tools available in the synchronous environment. Chapter 9 discuses how you can create synchronous exercises using tools available outside of the online classroom. After each tool is introduced and design guidelines are provided, the individual chapters provide sample instructional exercises and interactions that you can modify and incorporate into your own programs. Exercise set-up, screen design, objectives, and sample illustrations are provided.

About Pfeiffer

Pfeiffer serves the professional development and hands-on resource needs of training and human resource practitioners and gives them products to do their jobs better. We deliver proven ideas and solutions from experts in HR development and HR management, and we offer effective and customizable tools to improve workplace performance. From novice to seasoned professional, Pfeiffer is the source you can trust to make yourself and your organization more successful.

Essential Knowledge Pfeiffer produces insightful, practical, and comprehensive materials on topics that matter the most to training and HR professionals. Our Essential Knowledge resources translate the expertise of seasoned professionals into practical, how-to guidance on critical workplace issues and problems. These resources are supported by case studies, worksheets, and job aids and are frequently supplemented with CD-ROMs, websites, and other means of making the content easier to read, understand, and use.

Essential Tools Pfeiffer's Essential Tools resources save time and expense by offering proven, ready-to-use materials—including exercises, activities, games, instruments, and assessments—for use during a training or team-learning event. These resources are frequently offered in looseleaf or CD-ROM format to facilitate copying and customization of the material.

Pfeiffer also recognizes the remarkable power of new technologies in expanding the reach and effectiveness of training. While e-hype has often created whizbang solutions in search of a problem, we are dedicated to bringing convenience and enhancements to proven training solutions. All our e-tools comply with rigorous functionality standards. The most appropriate technology wrapped around essential content yields the perfect solution for today's on-the-go trainers and human resource professionals.

Live and Online!

Tips, Techniques, and Ready-to-Use Activities for the Virtual Classroom

Jennifer Hofmann

A Wiley Imprint
www.pfeiffer.com

Published by Pfeiffer
An Imprint of Wiley.
989 Market Street, San Francisco, CA 94103-1741 www.pfeiffer.com

For additional copies/bulk purchases of this book in the U.S. please contact 800-274-4434.

Pfeiffer books and products are available through most bookstores. To contact Pfeiffer directly call our Customer Care Department within the U.S. at 800-274-4434, outside the U.S. at 317-572-3985 or fax 317-572-4002 or visit www.pfeiffer.com.

Pfeiffer also publishes its books in a variety of electronic formats. Some content that appears in print may not be available in electronic books.

Printed in the United States of America

ISBN: 0-7879-6978-8

Library of Congress Cataloging-in-Publication Data

Acquiring Editor: *Martin Delahoussaye*
Director of Development: *Kathleen Dolan Davies*
Developmental Editor: *Susan Rachmeler*
Editor: *Rebecca Taff*
Senior Production Editor: *Dawn Kilgore*
Manufacturing Supervisor: *Bill Matherly*
Cover Design: *Michael Cook*

Illustrations:
Printed in the United States of America
Printing 10 9 8 7 6 5 4 3

Contents

CD-ROM Contents

Preface

In my book, *The Synchronous Trainer's Survival Guide*, I discussed in detail the specialized set of facilitation and delivery skills required to effectively teach in a live online (a.k.a. "synchronous") environment. Being able to communicate without body language and eye contact can be very challenging for a trainer accustomed to the traditional stand-up environment, and developing the skills necessary to master the synchronous classroom takes time and practice.

I also discussed the need for giving participants new skills so that they can also be successful in the online environment. How should they behave? How should they communicate? What should they expect?

So, in essence, the *Survival Guide* was focused on the behaviors and characteristics of the key actors on the virtual classroom stage—the trainer, the assistant trainer, and the participant. Looking back, I feel as if I "put the chicken before the egg." While it's fine to talk about how to interact successfully, shouldn't we first ascertain whether the participants have an environment in which they can learn and that the trainer is delivering content that is engaging and instructionally sound?

This introduces a new set of issues—specifically, questions dealing with instructional design and appropriate tool usage. This book, *Live and Online! Tips, Techniques, and Ready-to-Use Activities for the Virtual Classroom*, will discuss creating effective environments in which participants can be engaged and instructionally sound exercises that allow geographically dispersed participants to collaborate, interact, and, most importantly, to learn.

Motivation Behind the Book

Why a book specifically focused on creating collaborative synchronous exercises? That's an easy question—because it was needed. Attention so far has been focused on the point and click of the technology and individual tools.

(You can do "this" with application sharing and "that" with the whiteboard. . . . blah blah blah. . . .) There has not been a lot of attention paid to the instructional uses of the tools. I was frustrated with seeing tools underexploited. With just a little bit of creativity and the application of instructional design, programs can be much more interactive and collaborative. Interactive and collaborative programs help people to learn. Technology just provides the tools that facilitate this process. This book is just an early step in establishing models and best practices for synchronous exercise design and effective synchronous programs.

Acknowledgments

Thank you to the following synchronous training vendors for allowing the use of screen shots from their products to illustrate points throughout this book:

- Centra and the CentraOne™ product (www.centra.com)
- EDT Learning and the LearnLinc™ product (www.learnlinc.com)
- Elluminate and the vClass™ product (www.elluminate.com)
- HorizonLive and the HorizonLive™ product (www.horizonlive.com)
- Interwise and the Interwise Millenium™ product (www.interwise.com)
- Microsoft and the Microsoft Office Live Meeting (formerly PlaceWare) product (www.placeware.com)

When writing this book, I asked my synchronous colleagues for ideas that have been proven to work in the synchronous classroom. The following people responded with their ideas: Kathy Reinke, James Mowry, Elizabeth Tracy, Vikki Hollett, and Rog Hiemstra. Some industry publications and websites also provided the basis for some ideas. These are included in Appendix G.

Special thanks to Margaret Driscoll at IBM Lotus Software and Curtis Rockey of Rockey & Associates (www.RockTeam.com) for providing so much information around the topic of "Best Practices for Using Application Sharing," and to Nanette Miner for assistance with developing the instructor and participant guide samples.

October 2003 Jennifer Hofmann

Introduction

Like every innovation, learning technologies are a mixed blessing. They allow us to present content in many different formats and deliver that content to widely dispersed audiences at a relatively low cost. The potential impact is immense—technology is providing opportunities for people to learn when they may never have had the opportunity before. But technology-based learning initiatives present problems as well. Best practices are not well-documented, and success stories are more often linked to a return on investment based on the audience size and reduction of travel-related costs rather than to the effective impact of the program and mastery of the learning objectives. There seems to be an expectation that the technology will do the work for us. We either "dump" existing content onto the web without re-examining the validity of the content or exercises, or we delegate course creation to technology folks who incorporate every possible whiz-bang interaction available and create a program that is high-tech but not instructionally sound. Fundamentals like content validation and instructional design take a back seat to either aggressive project plans or technical wizardry.

Too often, the result is ineffective.

And ineffective training can have disastrous results. At the fundamental level, participants don't learn what they need to know—or they learn a minimal amount and believe they have mastered the content because they have completed the program. Often, the technology takes the blame for a lack of planning and design. Training professionals, not wanting the failure of a program to impact their personal credibility, are often very willing to further this belief rather than to take the blame for a program gone awry.

Sometimes it is the technology that is lacking, but the reality is that most content can be taught effectively at some level in an online environment. The key is designing effective interactions and ensuring that participants have all the tools they need to learn online.

This book is intended for instructional designers, subject-matter experts, or anyone who needs to design an event for the synchronous classroom. Online trainers should also consider this book, because they are often responsible for designing their own events and/or designing new exercises "on-the-fly" during a live event. Training managers and course sponsors will find this book helpful for understanding what it takes to design a synchronous program in terms of time and resources. This should be a team initiative. Reviewing at least the early chapters in this book will help the project team understand the realities of designing a synchronous program and help to break down the concept that the synchronous classroom is a "plug-and-play" medium—it takes planning, resources, and time to make it work.

Used ineffectively, the synchronous classroom can easily become as passive an experience as watching reruns on television—where the audience half listens and isn't concerned about becoming disengaged. The ultimate goal of this book is to help ensure that synchronous learning is an engaging and collaborative experience, more akin to a hands-on workshop than to network television.

How This Book Is Organized

The first three chapters of this book are focused on instructional design, creating effective learning environments, and online collaboration. Chapters 4 through 8 are concerned with specific collaboration tools available in the synchronous environment. Chapter 9 discusses how you can create synchronous exercises using tools available outside of the online classroom. After each tool is introduced and design guidelines are provided, the individual chapters provide sample instructional exercises and interactions that you can modify and incorporate into your own programs. Exercise set-up, screen design, script, instructions, objectives, and sample illustrations are provided.

Chapter 1—Designing for the Synchronous Classroom. This chapter provides instructional and slide design guidelines for synchronous course development. Also included are discussions on the changing role of the instructional designer and what topics can be taught in the synchronous classroom environment. Synchronous events as part of a blended design are introduced as a critical success factor. Finally, a list of instructional design tips is provided.

Chapter 2—Creating Successful Online Learning Environments. Just designing the right content isn't enough. Instructional designers also need to make sure the participants' learning environments are conducive to learning. This chapter examines the four factors critical to creating successful participant learning environments: participant motivation, opportunities to collaborate and interact, usable technology, and an active and participative trainer.

Chapter 3—An Overview of Synchronous Collaboration. Everyone talks about creating collaborative online environments, but what does online collaboration really mean? How are trainers and participants prepared to teach and learn online? Which online tools promote and encourage collaboration and why? This chapter will address these questions.

Chapters 4 through 8. Each addresses a different tool, provides sample exercises for that tool, and reviews alternatives for tools with different levels of capabilities.

- Chapter 4—Whiteboard
- Chapter 5—Chat
- Chapter 6—Breakout Room
- Chapter 7—Application Sharing
- Chapter 8—Synchronized Web Browsing

Chapter 9—Other Tools to Support Your Synchronous Programs. Don't limit yourself to the synchronous classroom during a live event! There are other, less obvious tools that you can use to support your program. This chapter explores some of these tools.

At the end of each exercise, there is room for you to take notes on how you may be able to customize the interaction for your specific projects. Make sure you keep track of the new ways you find to use the tools to collaborate online.

The Appendices contain important information that you can use immediately, including:

- Appendix A—A list of synchronous vendors and their contact information
- Appendix B—A detailed overview of the collaboration and facilitation features available in most synchronous training platforms that includes suggestions for instructional applications for each feature
- Appendix C—A checklist of considerations when designing for the synchronous classroom
- Appendix D—A completed Interactivity Plan illustrating the flow of a program
- Appendix E—Sample synchronous Leader Guide (excerpt)
- Appendix F—Sample synchronous Participant Guide (excerpt)
- Appendix G—Resources for instructional design, collaboration, and e-learning
- Appendix H—A glossary of e-learning terminology

The CD that accompanies this book contains sample graphics and leader guide pages that support the exercises explained in Chapters 4 through 8. You can import these pages directly into your materials. Templates for creating leader materials, participant materials, and Interactivity Plans are also available.

Finally, a web page has been developed (www.insynctraining.com/vendortools) that contains an up-to-date list of synchronous software vendors and specific information about the collaboration tools packaged with each platform.

There is a feedback form at the end of the book. I encourage you to use that form to compile all of your questions and send them to me. I will be happy to help you—and potentially incorporate the answers and your ideas into the next edition of this book.

Preparation

If you have never attended a synchronous session before, I strongly suggest you attend one or two prior to reading the book, and especially before putting what you read in this book into action. It will help you to visualize the environment and give you some context for the recommendations I make. If courses are offered within your organization, start there. If not, go to the website of your synchronous vendor and enroll in one or more public courses being offered.

A Note About Terminology

The focus of this book is designing collaborative synchronous exercises. "Synchronous" refers to programs that are delivered live over the Internet, or "live and online." In the context of this book, a "virtual classroom" is a specific software platform that supports synchronous instruction. (Appendix A contains a list of software vendors and their contact information.)

For the purpose of consistency, I have chosen specific words throughout this guide. For instance, I use the term "trainer" throughout, whereas you might use "instructor" or "teacher." I use the word "participant," but you might use "learner" or "student."

You will also notice that I use the term "learning technologies" instead of "training technologies" and "learning event" instead of "training event." This helps me to reinforce the reason I am in this industry: to create environments in which participants can learn. I believe that the learning outcome should be foremost in our minds; the delivery method is simply a means to an end.

"Designer" means different things to different people. For example, you can have instructional designers, graphic designers, or software designers. For the purposes of this book, "designer" in a standalone context refers to an "instructional designer."

Please refer to the glossary (Appendix H) at the end of this guide to clarify any terms with which you may not be familiar.

Starting Out . . .

As the field of online learning continues to evolve, and trainers and participants become more skilled in facilitating in the synchronous classroom, the exercise design process will become more sophisticated and the expectation levels of our audiences will be elevated. Keep that in mind as you design. This book should be used as a starting point. Use the sample exercises as models, and refine them to meet your needs. I'd love to hear about your ideas—and perhaps even incorporate them into the next edition!

1

Designing for the Synchronous Classroom

I remember being introduced to the process of instructional systems design (ISD) over a decade ago. I was working in a corporate training department of 40+ people, and all of us had spent quite a bit of time developing training classes of various types. Out of the blue, the word came down that we were all to learn a "systematic approach to program development." Well, they might as well have said that we needed to learn a new way to breathe. How dare they imply that we didn't know how to create a training program?! We had been successful so far, hadn't we? I was very worried because my style is not one that lends itself to a lot of structure and I felt that I would not be able to succeed with a dictated process.

They locked us in a room for ten hours (all 40+ of us) and gave us the overview of ISD. Then we all needed to go off and use the process to develop a project. Surprisingly (to me anyway), I embraced the process and became a convert. More than that, I am often considered "over the top" when it comes to applying a systematic approach to design of synchronous programs.

Instructional design is a critical component of creating a successful synchronous program. Applying a systematic process of design will help to ensure that your participants are learning, even though the trainer cannot physically see them.

There are many instructional design models. Some are much more detailed than others, but all have a level of applicability to designing for the synchronous classroom. A common model called the ADDIE mode is composed of five high-level steps, listed below and expanded on in Figure 1.1.

- Analyze—Identify the probable causes for a performance gap
- Design—Verify the desired learning objectives, the learning tasks, and the appropriate testing strategies.

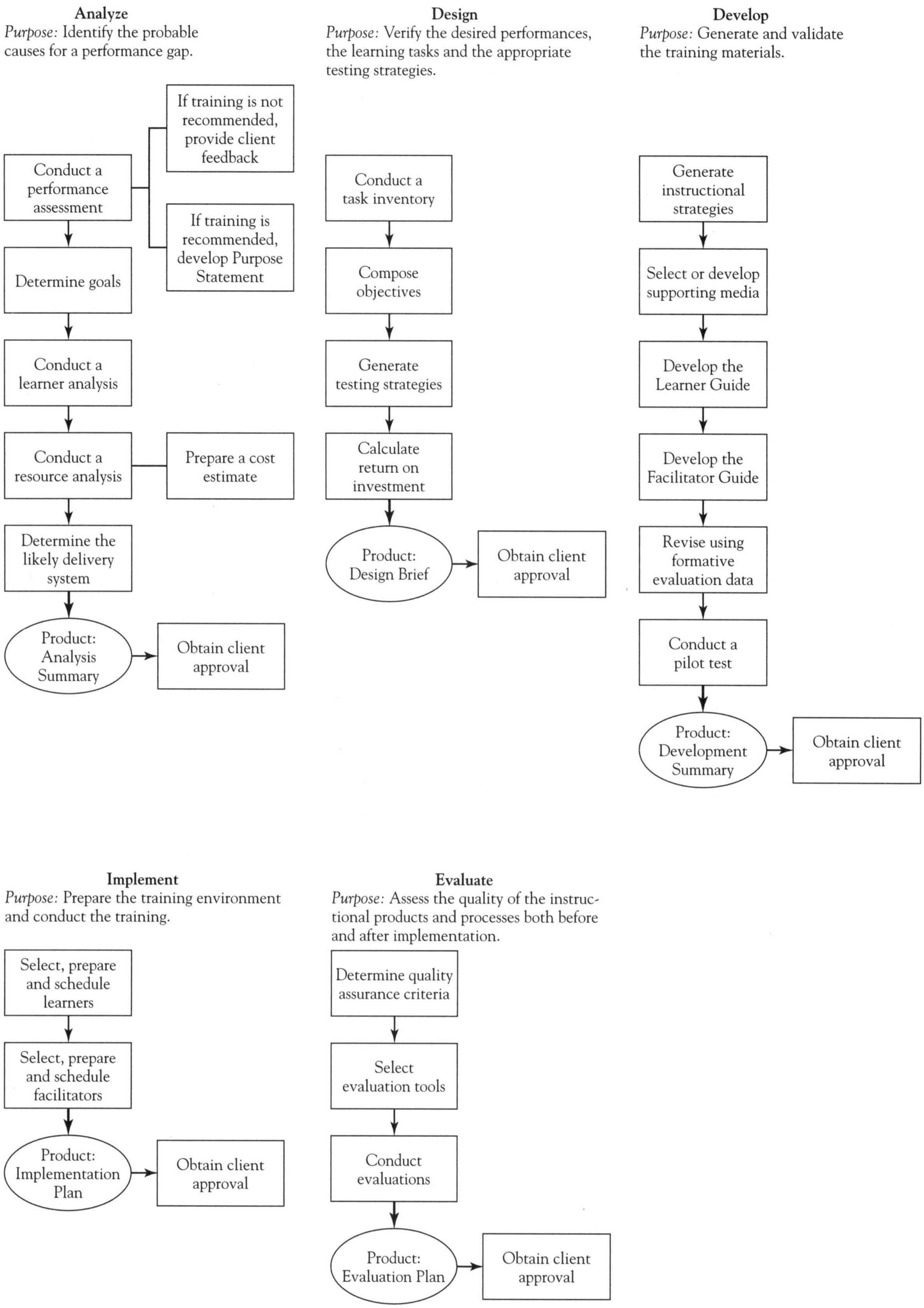

Analyze

Purpose: Identify the probable causes for a performance gap.

Conduct a performance assessment

If training is not recommended, provide client feedback

If training is recommended, develop Purpose Statement

Determine goals

Conduct a learner analysis

Conduct a resource analysis

Prepare a cost estimate

Determine the likely delivery system

Product: Analysis Summary

Obtain client approval

Design

Purpose: Verify the desired performances, the learning tasks and the appropriate testing strategies.

Conduct a task inventory

Compose objectives

Generate testing strategies

Calculate return on investment

Product: Design Brief

Obtain client approval

Develop

Purpose: Generate and validate the training materials.

Generate instructional strategies

Select or develop supporting media

Develop the Learner Guide

Develop the Facilitator Guide

Revise using formative evaluation data

Conduct a pilot test

Product: Development Summary

Obtain client approval

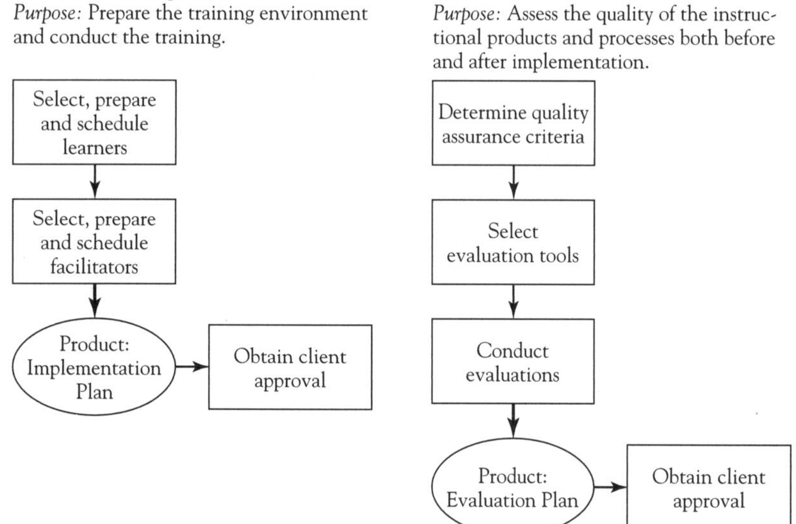

FIGURE 1.1 The Expanded ADDIE Model.

- Develop—Generate and validate the training materials.
- Implement—Prepare the training environment and conduct the training.
- Evaluate—Assess the quality of the instructional products and processes both before and after implementation.

I find that if I can get my customers to sit down for a day-long design session to determine the correct performance objectives, associated test items, and associated evaluation criteria, the rest of the process comes easily. There is plenty of content to be incorporated in most situations, but it's applying it properly that makes a good program.

Most of this book is focused on *designing* and *developing* effective synchronous exercises. (Instructional design resources are available in Appendix G.)

The Importance of Instructional Design in Web-Based Training

While most training professionals will agree that applying instructional design when developing courseware is important and results in a better program, it is rarely applied effectively. The amount of time that it takes to conduct an in-depth needs analysis, systematically apply instructional design, and revise instruction based on evaluation feedback is seen by most project sponsors as excessive. The process is also considered to be expensive—especially the evaluation and revision stage. Management expects that the program will be right the first time.

Instructional designers have found many ways to short-cut the process in order to make up for the lack of time and resources. They make their best guesses, create materials, and hope for the chance to sit in on early course deliveries so they can use them as an unofficial pilot class and be able to update the design and materials based on their observations.

Fortunately, the traditional stand-up training environment provides quite a bit of flexibility and room for creativity. A skilled trainer, familiar with the program content, can often compensate for a faulty design. Changing exercises, shortening breaks, and making determinations about which content is the most appropriate to deliver based on the group of participants in front of them is an exercise most trainers perform automatically. When a program is managed successfully, participants often do not notice design flaws.

e-Learning, both asynchronous (self-directed with or without a trainer) and synchronous (real-time), are less forgiving delivery platforms than the traditional classroom. When an exercise doesn't work, it is often immediately obvious to the participant. In asynchronous programs, the trainer is not able to observe the breakdown of the process, and participants are left struggling to compensate for the weak design. While synchronous trainers have more opportunities to try different exercises, the short periods of time available are very limiting. For example, trainers cannot cancel lunch or shorten breaks. Typical synchronous sessions are one to two hours in length. Because of this, synchronous participants are not very forgiving of a program that ends 15 or 30 minutes past the scheduled time. Worse, synchronous trainers do not have the benefit of eye contact and body language to alert them that participants are having problems understanding or applying content. Unless a true assessment plan is part of the process, the trainer may walk away thinking that successful knowledge transfer has occurred, when in reality participants are left confused.

An unsuccessful e-learning program can impact the organization in several ways. Most apparently, participants are left without the knowledge and skills required to do some aspect of their jobs. Resources that could have been applied toward a more successful initiative were wasted. Training professionals, not eager to have dispersions cast on their own credibility, may be ready and willing to support the idea that the technologies were not appropriate for the content. While some objectives may not lend themselves to online instruction, too often technology is blamed for the lack of planning and design on the part of the course development team.

As an instructional designer, I know that the application of the ISD process always results in a better program, *but it is much more important in e-learning initiatives*. Look back at web courses that failed in your organization. Can you identify design flaws that affected the course? Try to document and learn from those mistakes.

Common Design Problems and Suggested Solutions

Instructional designers new to the field of synchronous training technologies often make the mistake of assuming that synchronous classrooms are simply re-creations of traditional classroom settings. All the familiar elements seem to be present—most notably a live trainer and an audience participating in real-time. They (instructional designers) are given some basic guidelines: make it interactive, teach in one- or two-hour increments, try to use the technology, and so on. And do it fast!

The most common mistake new synchronous instructional designers make is to not participate in many, indeed any, synchronous programs. Traditional programs are converted to fit into the assigned time periods (one hour, ninety minutes, or whatever). Content and exercises are dropped (dumped!!) online with little thought given to how those exercises will work online. In reality, the synchronous medium is very different from traditional programs. Because participants are geographically dispersed and trainers cannot rely on body language and eye contact, exercises need to be redesigned to maximize engagement and facilitate the transfer of knowledge. One of the necessary preparatory steps for instructional designers new to the synchronous medium is to attend as many online programs as possible so that they understand the experience of the online participant. Concurrently, designers need to be given the opportunity to learn as much about their synchronous platform as possible. It is not enough, for example, to know that a "whiteboard" is available. They need to know the particular characteristics of a specific whiteboard. For example, "What drawing tools can be used?" or "How many people can write on the whiteboard at once?" Once the participant experience and the technology are mastered, the instructional designer is much better prepared to create effective synchronous courseware.

A list of synchronous tools, their instructional uses, and questions to ask about them, can be found in Appendix B.

Another common mistake made when creating synchronous content is the overuse of PowerPoint® content. (PowerPoint is the tool most widely utilized for the creation of synchronous content. After a slide show has been created in the presentation software, it is imported into the learning environment using the synchronous platform's course assembly function.) Slides are packed with bulleted data. The problem with this approach to data creation is that screens become too "busy." Participants, after taking a minute to read the screen, tend to "tune out" the trainer's voice and concentrate on the bullet points. Any additional commentary or stories provided by the trainer seem not to be as important as what is preprinted on the slides. This can cause an additional problem. New synchronous trainers, unsure of how to facilitate in this new environment, have a tendency to rush through the reading of content-heavy slides and create an environment in which interaction is minimized. Slides should be created with a minimum of words and should instead have concepts, questions, and/or graphics that encourage conversation, as shown in the sample slides in Figure 1.2.

Sometimes designers try to use the technology inappropriately. For example, one organization that I worked with had a strict guideline that a poll needed to be incorporated into a synchronous course at least every five minutes. (In this context, a poll was a multiple-choice question designed—theoretically—to test comprehension.) This met their minimum

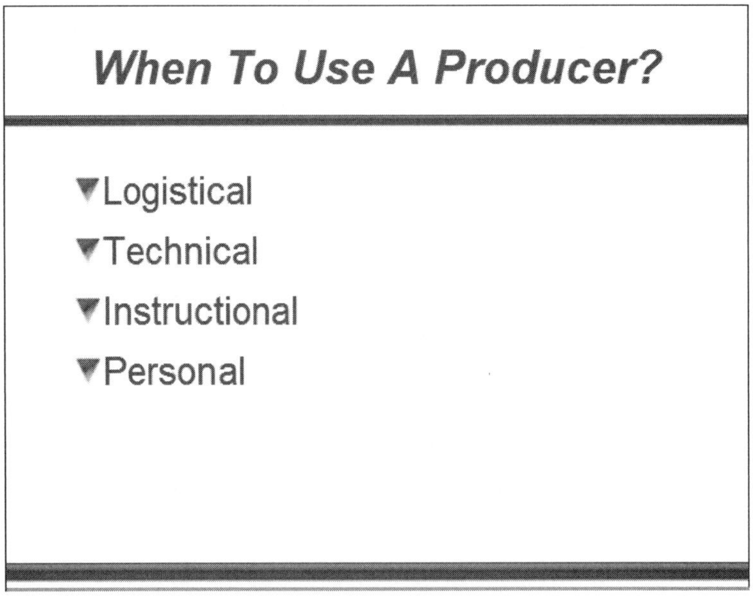

When To Use A Producer?
▼Logistical
▼Technical
▼Instructional
▼Personal

Well Designed

When To Use A Producer?
Deciding when and how to use a producer is based on many factors:
Logistical: Is there another person available to act as a producer? Does the budget allow for this person?
Technical: Does your software platform support an "assistant" of some sort? If not, what can someone logged in as participant do to assist?
Instructional: Do the design and desired outcomes require an assistant?
Personal: Do you find yourself thinking, "I don't use an assistant in the traditional classroom – why do I need one now?"

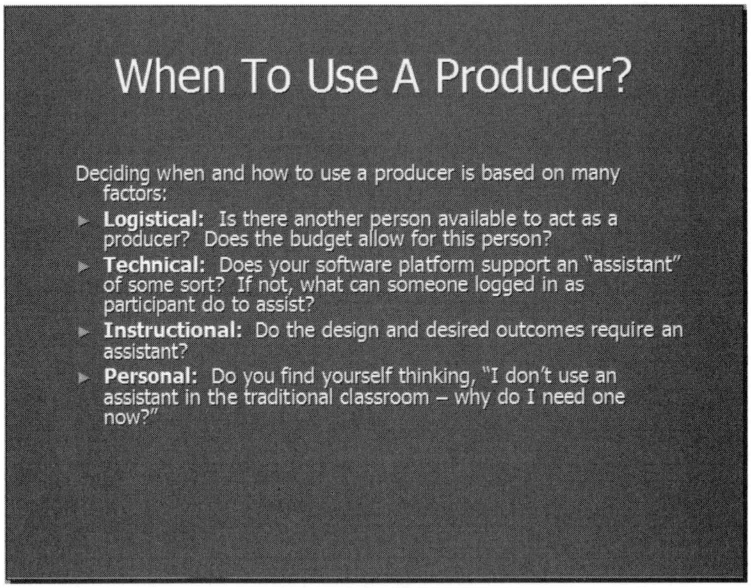

Poorly Designed

FIGURE 1.2 Two Sample Slides.

requirement for how they defined participant interaction, but did not consider whether or not a polling question made sense from a design perspective or whether another interaction might be more appropriate. A sample is shown in Figure 1.3.

To this group, polling the audience satisfied the need for interaction in the program. Instead of arbitrarily creating rules for tool use, the designer should consider the objectives of each exercise and incorporate the tools to support the content and objectives. Don't let the medium become the message!

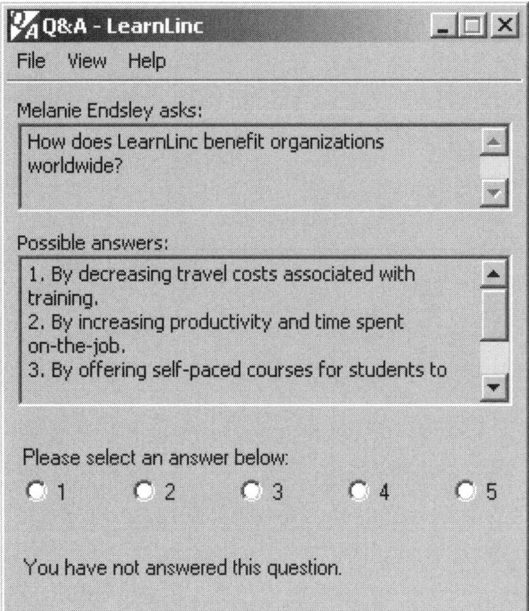

FIGURE 1.3 Sample of a LearnLinc Polling Question.

The *design phase* is often best accomplished by a team. When a group, prepared with a completed analysis and a set of validated learning objectives (and, of course, an understanding of the available tools!), can sit down and brainstorm the most effective ways to deliver the content, the result is often collaborative, engaging, and instructionally sound exercises.

What Can Be Taught Online?

Two general categories of online training are *synchronous* and *asynchronous*. Each methodology has its representative tools. Synchronous delivery systems include real-time interactive tools like chat, whiteboarding, two-way voice, and application sharing. Asynchronous delivery systems include facilitated collaborative tools that students can use at a time that is convenient for them (like discussion boards and email) and self-directed, non-collaborative tools that rely on the participant completing coursework without feedback or interaction.

While it is often easily accepted that technologies (desktop and Internet applications) can be taught online, there is often resistance to moving so-called "business skills" or "soft skills" to the synchronous environment. Trainers who have been delivering leadership skills, for example, often have doubts about the effectiveness of delivering such dynamic content via the online classroom.

So what can be taught online? To answer this question about a particular program, I suggest looking at the individual learning objectives. (Remember, you create the learning objectives during the design stage of the process, after your analysis has been completed.) After you write your objectives, answer these questions for each individual objective:

1. Is the audience geographically dispersed or co-located?

   If the audience is co-located, then online training may not be necessary. Live classroom programs may be more appropriate.

2. Is the content unstable?

   If the content is unstable and expected to continue to change, developing asynchronous programs may not be economically realistic because of the time and expense involved in programming interactive asynchronous modules. Synchronous programs may still be a good option because you can easily update slides to accommodate new content.

3. Will this program be taught repeatedly over a long period of time or delivered just a few times?

   If you only expect to deliver the content a few times, developing asynchronous programs may not be economically realistic because of the time and expense involved in programming interactive asynchronous modules.

4. Does the participant need to have real-time access to an expert or a trainer in order to learn the content effectively? Why or why not?

   Requiring real-time access to an expert or trainer eliminates asynchronous training from your options.

5. If real-time access to an expert or a trainer is required, can that person teach from a distance? Why or why not?

   There are situations when an expert must be present to demonstrate a skill or a trainer must be present to test a participant. If you can justify why this physical presence is required, then you may not be able to teach that particular objective online.

6. Would collaboration and/or discussion between participants substantially enhance the learning? Why or why not?

   If collaboration and/or discussion would not enhance the experience, you probably have content that is best delivered in an asynchronous environment. Since it is difficult to keep the attention of the synchronous participant, any content that would result in lectures longer than ten minutes should probably be delivered asynchronously. This could mean a reading assignment, a tutorial, or some kind of recording. If collaboration and/or discussion would enhance the experience, create synchronous events that are supplemented by asynchronous content distribution.

7. Can you test the objectives in an online environment?

   Even if the answers to all of the previous questions indicate the possibility of online content delivery, you need to make sure you can test mastery of the objective in an online environment. You may be able to teach content, discuss problems, and collaborate online, but find a different way to test for mastery.

It is vital that each learning objective be considered individually. The instructional designer should not look at a program from the global level. It may be determined that most of the objectives can be taught online, but one or two could require a different approach. That's when the designer can start to determine the appropriate blend, or mix, of learning technologies for the program.

Applying a Blended Delivery Method

Blending synchronous and asynchronous technologies together is important for several reasons. First, consider that your participants may learn in different ways. Some may need time to process information and review content independently before responding. These participants may enjoy learning in the asynchronous mode. Others may prefer a live approach, in which ideas and feedback can be quickly exchanged. For this group, some kind of synchronous technology may be the most effective. For any instructional medium or program, creating a program that is 100 percent entrenched in one technology or the other can easily disenfranchise some participants. Therefore, online programs should include both asynchronous and synchronous interactions in order to be most effective.

Let's look at a simplified example. Suppose you were asked to design a program that taught new trainers traditional classroom presentation skills. If you made a decision based on just that information, you probably would decide that the content was not appropriate for an online presentation. But let's look at some potential individual learning objectives for this program.

At the end of the program, participants will be able to:

1. Complete a thorough audience analysis;
2. Prepare and organize an effective presentation;
3. Identify effective presentation skills;
4. Use visual aids in an effective manner; and

5. Demonstrate the characteristics and competencies of an effective stand-up presenter.

Objectives 1, 2, and 3 can be easily taught online because the content is stable, the program will probably be taught repeatedly, and the trainer can teach these objectives from a distance.

Objectives 4 and 5 need to be managed differently. Because these objectives cannot be tested in an online format, another way for the participants to demonstrate mastery must be found. Perhaps participants have to gather together to make their final presentations, reducing a potential three-day program to one day. Perhaps a videotape sent to the trainer for evaluation would help to meet this requirement.

Once you have gone through this process, you can make some decisions about how to obtain the right "blend" for your program.

"Nice to Know" vs. "Need to Know" Content in the Synchronous Classroom

When a traditional stand-up program is designed, it often includes content that falls into the "nice to know" category. This is because there is often a surplus of time and the flexibility to make determinations on how to use it. If a particular topic takes longer than expected, the trainer can decide to eliminate some "nice to know" content.

The synchronous environment does not provide that same flexibility. Designers must make sure that all the content in the short synchronous session falls into the "need to know" category. The session should be supported by reading assignments or web pages that contain the "nice-to-know" information; trainers should let participants know how to access these resources and when/why they might decide to use that information.

Distinguishing "Prework" from "Real Work"

No matter how effective and well-designed a prework assignment is, many participants do not take the time to thoroughly complete the work. Often, they don't even review it prior to a learning event. In our training culture there is a tendency to believe that if the content is important enough, the trainer will cover it in class. Trainers often reinforce this behavior by covering the major points for anyone who did not happen to complete the prework.

With blended learning technologies that include short, synchronous events, we (training professionals) need to create a culture in which work assigned outside of live events is completed and taken seriously. We must migrate from "prework" to "real work," where self-paced exercises are a critical part of the learning process. Trainers simply do not have the time to reteach content that should have been learned prior to the class. Synchronous classroom time should be used for clarification, questions, collaboration, and application—all based on the asynchronous work completed prior to the live event.

This is a huge cultural shift for participants. To accommodate this, designers have to set clear expectations concerning what learners must accomplish before attending class. To ensure completion, trainers may do several things: send out an email message; ask participants to answer questions posted on a discussion board; or have participants email the commentary to the trainer to verify that the asynchronous assignment was completed. If a participant does not complete the verification process, the trainer may decide not to provide the password to attend the live online event. It is critical that organizations implement this culture change early and enforce its guidelines.

One of the benefits of synchronous programs is that, since participants aren't traveling to a classroom, they haven't wasted any time if you tell them they cannot attend a session. Trainers can simply send an email note with a schedule of upcoming sessions and indicate that the participant can enroll for any of them once he or she has had the opportunity to complete the asynchronous portion of the program.

The designers must make certain that, once participants get to the live event, the fact that they have completed the self-directed work activities is recognized. This will ensure that participants feel that every part of the learning process is worthwhile and will encourage them to complete the self-directed work prior to future synchronous events. Knowledge tests, discussions, and verbal acknowledgments early in the live session are all effective ways to reinforce the fact that completing the assignments was a valuable use of time.

Instructional Materials

A critical outcome of the instructional design process is the production of instructional materials. Just because you are using a synchronous classroom as a delivery tool doesn't mean paper materials can be totally eliminated.

Leader guides, participant guides, and slides are examples of instructional materials that should be used to support the synchronous environment. While slides are almost always part of the mix, leader guides and participant guides are often overlooked completely. Trainers depend on the slide content to prompt them through the program, and copies of PowerPoint slides pass as participant materials.

Using Your Leader Guide Effectively

For some reason, when trainers start teaching synchronously, they often decide not to use a leader guide. If you want your online programs to be as interactive and "high touch" as they are in the traditional classroom, using leader guides becomes even more important. Written effectively, leader guides capture the choreography of the program, documenting what the trainer, the producer, the participants, and the technology are doing. Since they are often all doing something different at the same time (sometimes even multiple things!), you should have a detailed plan that explains the design. If you do not, you may discover that your event is much more lecture-oriented than you wanted and that interaction with participants is limited to "yes/no" questions and a few polls.

Optimally, you will be teaching your synchronous classes from some sort of guide or syllabus. These can vary from task descriptions and checklists to detailed scripts. What you should use depends largely on your personal preference; some synchronous trainers find highly detailed leader guides too constraining, while others appreciate the security of explicit scripts. Appendix E provides a sample leader guide, and templates are available on the CD.

(*Note:* For leader guide design strategies, see Chapter 4 of *The Synchronous Trainer's Survival Guide*.)

Slide Design

Since, in most synchronous events, the participants cannot see each other or the trainer, the content on the screen has become the center of attention. It is critical that the slides be designed to keep the attention of the participant. I use the following guidelines when designing slides for synchronous events:

- *Use a white background and leave a lot of white space.* This allows the trainer to scribe on the slides using all of the whiteboard tools without worrying about the colors of the annotations. It also encourages participants to collaborate on the whiteboard if the exercise calls for that.
- *Keep bullets to a minimum.* If there are more than three or four bullet points, use multiple slides. This leaves the trainer more room to write and annotate. It also keeps the participants from reading too far ahead and assuming they understand the content. Remember, it's easy for participants to "check out" and stop listening. Don't give them a reason for it.

- *Make bullets highlighted points, not detailed content.* If there is too much detail on the screen, the trainer will be tempted to just read from the screen, and participants will wonder why they couldn't have just read the slides on their own time.
- *Use the screen for exercises, not content, whenever possible.* Using questions or exercise instructions on the screen gives the trainer the opportunity to engage participants. (Chapter 4, Whiteboard Exercises and Techniques, will provide detailed strategies for how to accomplish this.)

The Importance of Participant Guides

A well-designed participant guide can assist the trainer in facilitating small-group and independent exercises and increase the comfort level for participants not experienced in the synchronous classroom. A sample participant guide can be found in Appendix F, and templates can be found on the CD. (See Figure 1.4.)

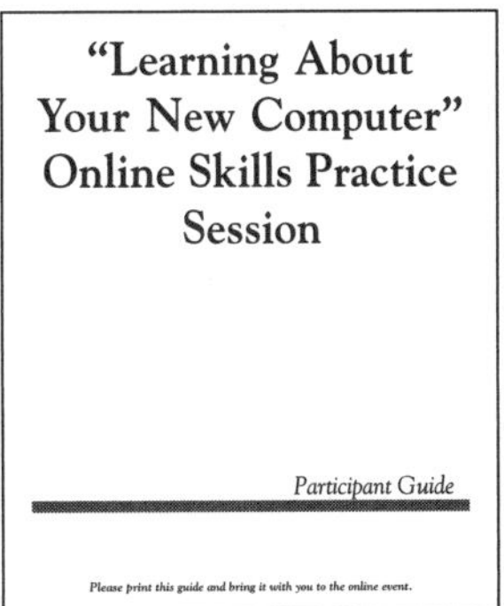

"Learning About Your New Computer" Online Skills Practice Session

Participant Guide

Please print this guide and bring it with you to the online event.

FIGURE 1.4 Participant Materials Are a Critical Component of a Collaborative Blend.

I have found that participants have a more difficult time understanding directions in a synchronous classroom, so it helps dramatically if you incorporate directions to all independent and small-group exercises into a participant guide. Before you have participants start an exercise, explain the directions and direct them to the appropriate page in the participant guide. Also remind them that you will be monitoring the private chat area so they can ask additional questions.

Avoid sending out PowerPoint slides that duplicate your presentation ahead of time. This is a sure way to disengage some of your participants. Many will tend to review the slides on paper and try to listen. If their eyes are on their desks, and not on the classroom, they will not be able to see the on-screen interactions and collaborations and will lose much of the value of the synchronous experience. Instead of replicating the screens, the participant guide should complement them and help to support class interactions. For example, instead of lecturing for five minutes around three bullet points on a screen, ask the participants to read about them in a participant guide article and then answer questions located at the end of the article in the chat area. Debrief their answers verbally and then move on to the next interaction.

(*Note:* For more information on working with participants in the synchronous classroom, see Chapter 6 of *The Synchronous Trainer's Survival Guide*.)

Assessment

Assessment is a critical component to any training program, delivered traditionally or online. Activities like pre-tests, embedded tests, post-tests, and course evaluations should be as critical to your synchronous program design as they are for your classroom program design. Because direct trainer observation of participants is not available with the loss of eye contact and body language, assessment of knowledge and skills transfer using testing devices may be even more important to ensure that learning actually took place. Use polls and feedback mechanisms throughout the live event to verify that individual points were understood and a final assessment of some kind (test, participant presentation, or follow-up written assignment) to verify that the event was successful.

Design Tips

To conclude, here are some general guidelines for instructional designers to keep in mind when designing synchronous programs.

- *Design in a group environment.* More people often bring more ideas to the table. When it comes to instructional design, the more minds the better! Even a short brainstorming session to review a draft design can improve your program.
- *Chunk and group your learning objectives.* Determine which objectives can be taught synchronously and which objectives require traditional or asynchronous approaches. Arrange these chunks into a blended learning solution using different technologies.

- *Enforce your blend.* Use a mixture of traditional, asynchronous, and synchronous technologies and find ways to ensure participants complete all of the components. Make learning a process, not an event. Find ways to ensure that asynchronous work is completed and valued.
- *Create interactions every three to five minutes.* It is easy for synchronous training to become all about the trainer and a passive experience for the participants. Without something to do every three to five minutes, participants can easily become disengaged. Chapters 4 through 9 provide detailed examples of activities that give participants "something to do." Designers should include timing references in leader materials to ensure that the designs meet this guideline.
- *Break up speeches with exercises and engaging discussions.* If a lecture is longer than five minutes, it is too long. If there is a substantial amount of lecture content, consider asynchronous approaches like reading materials or recordings of some kind.
- *Don't let the tools dictate the design.* It is easy to get caught up in using all of the tools that are available. Be careful because this shifts the focus away from content. Make sure your tools support your design rather than overwhelming it.
- *Find ways to keep everyone busy.* This book contains many examples of exercises that can engage all of the synchronous participants at the same time. This is a critical part of maintaining everyone's attention. When everyone can participate at the same time, you can be reasonably sure they aren't working on unrelated tasks, exercises take less time, and everyone's voice is heard. (Chapter 3 focuses on "synchronous collaboration" and expands on this point in detail.)
- *Include technical instructions, screen shots, and assistant trainer notes in your leader guides.* Remember, you may be designing for trainers who are new to the synchronous environment, and you must support them as much as possible.

(*Note:* For more information on the roles of the online trainer and assistant trainer, see Chapter 2 of *The Synchronous Trainer's Survival Guide*.)

- *Design participant materials; don't just distribute slides.* When participants have access to the exact slides as they can see on the screen, they will tend to look at the printed slides and miss the important interactions that occur in the synchronous environment. Create participant materials that supplement and support the program, but do not replicate the screens.

- *Pilot and revise*. Your exercises won't all work perfectly the first time. You'll need to test them in realistic environments before setting the instructions in stone. (For designers, synchronous deliveries offer a distinct advantage over their more traditional counterparts. Designers can log in and observe just about any class they want, without the time and expense associated with travel. They can also watch recordings of live sessions and use them to evaluate the effectiveness of exercises.)
- *Involve trainers early in the process*. Trainers often have insights into the intended audience's competency levels, access to technology, and tolerance for "games" and other types of instructional exercises.
- *Design with realistic technology expectations*. Instructional designers often have high-end computers on a dedicated internal network and they don't understand how their training will work in "the field."

Well-designed content isn't the only indicator of success. Organizations need to look at the learning environments of participants and make certain they are conducive to success. Chapter 2 looks at motivation, collaboration opportunities, technology, and the online trainer as critical success factors in the online learning environment.

2

Creating Successful Online Learning Environments

We all know that online learning has gone beyond being a trend and has become an accepted and permanent part of our teaching mix. It is hard to come up with a subject that is not, in some form and at some level, taught online. Whether it's astronomy or zoology, Arabic or Zulu, addition or . . . well, you see where I'm going with this. If you want to learn about something, a simple Google search will get you started. Besides being plentiful, programs are low-priced or, often, free!

Organizations and training vendors are very motivated to place content online. Ease of distribution and the relatively low cost of production (compared to a comparable traditional program) are resulting in online and blended solutions becoming part of almost every organization's training plan.

So with all of this content available at such an affordable price, why aren't more people learning online? And why are so many of those who are learning online being forced to do so by their managers at a metaphorical gunpoint?

The answer, I think, is easy to identify. While organizations are spending money on technology and programming, they are often not investing in creating effective learning environments to encourage participants' success. We are treating e-learning implementations as technology initiatives instead of as change initiatives. We must find ways to make e-learning "real learning"—and ensure that participants understand that the energy invested is worthwhile.

To ensure that participants are successful, organizations should make sure that the following characteristics are present in their learning environments:

- Adequate participant motivation;
- Opportunity for participants to collaborate and interact;

- Useable technology; and
- An active and participative trainer.

During the analysis phase of the ISD process, the designer should investigate the environment and identify to what extent these critical success factors can be incorporated into the learning experience.

Participant Motivation

Everyone understands how to learn in a traditional classroom environment. We've been doing it all of our lives.

Online learning has introduced a new learning culture—one that takes time with which to become familiar. Organizations use a great deal of resources planning for and investing in technologies, but often forget about the culture change involved with this new learning environment. In order for online learning to be successful, developers need to create environments in which people can effectively learn. Participants need to be open to learning in this new way, and confident that their time invested in professional development is well-spent.

Why do we need to be more concerned about motivating online learners than traditional learners? It is because online learning often comes with a stigma that's totally unmotivating. Learners often feel that they're being cheated out of an instructor, that online learning isn't real learning, and that having to learn at their desk is more trouble then it is worth. While going to a traditional class may have interrupted the week, at least it gave us a change of environment—and usually there were snacks.

These demotivators are fairly obvious. Indeed, negative factors always seem to be the most recognizable when individuals are faced with a change.

Our challenge as e-learning professionals is to find ways to motivate learners so the demotivators become less of an issue.

Sources of Motivation

So, how do we motivate our online participants? Keep this list in mind when designing your online courses and interacting with your learners and you may be amazed at what a difference a little motivation makes.

- **Publish requirements and set expectations ahead of time.** Getting more work than you bargained for or taking a class that isn't appropriate isn't only demotivating, it can be downright aggravating. To ensure that learners are able to meet expectations, publish them ahead of time. Create a Webpage containing a detailed course description, learning objectives, work assignments, and an estimate of the time it will take to complete all of the work. Explain the technology mix and any prerequisite requirements. Armed with enough information, learners can make an informed choice about the appropriateness of the course for them. And if the course is required, at least individuals can try to balance their schedules to accommodate the workload.
- **Establish relevance.** Many organizations have libraries with hundreds of off-the shelf online learning programs. That's great, if the learners need the content. Before requiring someone to take a course (off-the-shelf or home grown), communicate the reasons why the content is import to the individual and the organization. If the learners don't understand the relevance, they will tend to the minimal amount necessary in order to complete the program.
- **Provide continuous encouragement.** Email and other communications are great, cheap, and easy ways to encourage your online learners. Post a Frequently Asked Questions list on a discussion board. Email reminders and offers of assistance, or personally call learners that aren't logging on. Knowing that a real person is watching over things helps to humanize the online environment, and motivates learners to stay engaged.
- **Use assessments.** Surprisingly, assessment has been identified as a key motivator for online learners. Participants learn what they know will be assessed.
- **Building in tests.** Requiring participation in discussion boards, or inviting supervisors to observe synchronous classes are all very effective techniques that are easy to implement. Publish the course requirements and assessment techniques, and let potential learners know that if they fail

to meet the minimum requirements at the end of the course, they will need to take the class again.

- **Get supervisor and peer support.** One of the most difficult parts about learning at your desks is the constant interruptions by those working around you. There's a perception that online learning can be interrupted, without much consequence. However, the reality is that once a learner is interrupted several times, retention falls and the number of learners who will complete the program dramatically lowers. Similarly, if a participant feels they need to work after-hours in order to complete a program, they'll grow to resent the medium. Learners should plan time to complete programs, inform their supervisors and peers, and should feel confident that the required time will be respected.
- **Market internally, market continuously.** In a networked world, word gets around fast. Make sure the word about online learning is positive, and constantly reinforced by people that matter. An initial marketing burst without a continuing campaign will make your initiative appear to be another passing fad. But regular news about what courses are coming up and their importance to the organization will help employees understand that online learning is an integral part of the organization's learning culture. If online learning is "in," employees will want to be part of the crowd.
- **Make learning a management mandate.** It's critical to have upper-level management support the idea that online learning is a vehicle for professional development in your organization. Get management involved by inviting them to record short presentations to welcome learners and encourage them to participate in the online initiative. If potential participants know that management is behind the initiative, they'll be more inclined to sign-up.
- **Offer rewards and recognition.** It feels great to answer a question correctly, and to receive feedback from instructors and peers. Learners often don't expect positive reinforcement from online courses. Find ways to build in opportunity for tangible rewards and recognition—even for asynchronous programs. Provide completion certificates and publish a regular report containing the names of people who successfully finished courses. You can also link online learning programs to the performance management process, making it clear to participants that the time they spend participating in online programs is recognized as contributing to their professional development.
- **Publicize success stories.** Early technology adaptors will try anything, the rest of us need a little coaxing. Finding and publishing success stories about online learning in your organization is a great way to reassure

tentative new learners that they can be successful learning online. Use the success stories to supplement your marketing effort.

- **Ensure personal success.** Give learners the opportunity to be successful and they will come back! Do your best to create effective online learning environments, strong support systems, and well-designed programs right from the beginning. More important, provide early successes and ground-roots support for the organizational initiative.

Collaboration and Interaction

Early computer-based training programs were represented by designs that were, by nature, independent studies. Partnered with the evolution of Internet technologies, computer-based programs have started to focus on more collaborative interactions, including the experiences and feedback of other participants in various asynchronous (self-directed) and synchronous (live and online) exercises.

How can online education be collaborative? When you find ways to bring participants together in some kind of social interaction or bring groups together to work to solve problems, you have potential collaboration. Participants in online programs feel more involved in the process, and therefore learn more effectively, when involved in these interactive collaborations. Chapter 3 discusses online collaboration in more detail.

Technology

Probably the most obvious impediment to learning online is the technology: software, hardware, bandwidth, and being able to use it all. When talking with people (learners, trainers, IT) about what they are worried about—technology is usually first on their list. The fourth critical success factor to creating effective, online learning environments is useable and accessible technology; however, useable and accessible technology means more than a system that operates. It means having technology that works efficiently, having support for that technology, having programs that are designed to effectively utilize the technology, and orienting learners to their new environment.

While technology is advancing all the time (for example, more bandwidth is available, hardware and software are becoming less expensive), there are still many issues that need to be addressed to ensure that learners have a positive online experience.

The first issue is just making sure that learner's technology works. Before they start doing work, they need to make sure that their technology works so that they have enough time to fix things or come up with other solutions. Typically, we send out hardware and software specification (i.e., RAM, bandwidth, operating system requirements), while this information is very useful to their technical support contact, it generally doesn't do the end user much good. To assist the end user, give them tips on how to test to see if they meet the minimum requirements. For example, if a sound card and speakers are required—give them a link to a website that has sound on it. Another thing that you can do to assist is to send them a set of questions that they can use to communicate with their desktop support, such as:

- Is my machine equipped with a sound card that allows for audio-in and audio-out
- What bandwidth do I have access to
- What plug-ins (Flash, RealPlayer, etc.) are standards or my machine
- What version browser am I using
- Are there any firewall issues (for instance if VoIP is used, or if there are website access restrictions).

Once the learner has verified that minimal technical requirements have been met, make sure that you provide them with contact information (phone number and email) in case they have technical problems while using the software (i.e., password issues, system crashes, or unexpected happenings).

Suggest that they print these instructions and post them in their learning area since it won't help to have the information in their computer if the computer goes down.

It is critical that learners test their machines well ahead of any scheduled online activity. Too often, the first clue that learners have that their machine isn't responding appropriately, is when they sit down to complete their assignment or attend the program. This can be too late to resolve the issue and results in a frustrating learning experience that will leave a lasting impact.

Learner Orientation

The next issue with which we need to be concerned is to make sure that learners can use the technology so effectively that collaboration becomes effortless. Even though many online software packages—both synchronous and asynchronous—are touted by the vendors as easy-to-use, we still need to give the participants the opportunity to acclimate themselves to this new learning environment.

I suggest some kind of online learning orientation program. Use the synchronous classroom (the live, online classroom) to manage this process and offer this orientation to your learners on a regular basis. During the program, give participants permission to be frustrated and ask them to share their frustrations during the class. You want to alleviate their frustrations here, and not let them carry over to content oriented programs.

In this orientation, consider including the following items:

- A tools overview, which instructs learners on how to use the different technologies that they will be using in the online class
- Communication guidelines that emphasize the importance of participating actively and completing all assignment
- Ground rules to instruct learners about what is acceptable and not acceptable in this new learning environment (for live events they need to show up early, self-directed work MUST be completed prior to live events, if they need to "step out" they need to inform the online facilitator, etc.)
- Provide participants tips on how they can maximize the learning experience from their own desk—how to minimize interruption, maintain focus and concentration, and how to communicate with their managers and peers that they are actively engaged in a learning process
- Explain the different components of the program—for example you may have an asynchronous discussion board supporting multiple live, online events, and this blend may be supplemented by a printed participant workbook with assignments that need to be completed by specific deadlines. Emphasize the fact that self-directed work is as important as any of the live events and that the learner needs to commit to the entire learner process.

It's not a bad idea to have your IT support team participate in online orientations and events so that they understand the environment they must support and can intelligently answer technical questions from learners. This insider experience also may make them more empathetic to the time-is-of-the-essence pressure the learner faces.

Bells and Whistles Don't Make Learning

Another thing that we can do to minimize the focus on the technology rather than the learning, happens at the design stage of the program. The instructional designer needs to resist incorporating all of the bells and whistles that the learning technology allows. Make sure that any use of technology supports the learning and is not showing off programming skills. For this reason it is very important the designer is involved with multimedia tutorials. Don't simply turn over the development to a programmer and assume that they are going to create the best environment. Sometimes simplicity makes the best point.

To help ensure that this occurs, it is critical that the instructional designer be familiar with the technology from the learner perspective. The instructor should participate in programs that have been constructed using the various technologies they will be using as well. For example, if the instructional designer determines that a self directed multi media tutorial is he best method for delivering a particular piece of content—they should take as many classes as possible that are in this format in order to identify best practices in exercise design, screen design, and navigation, and in keeping learners engaged. If it is determined that a live, online interaction is the best delivery medium, then they need to be sure they are familiar with all of the collaboration tools available in their synchronous platform. Additionally, they should attend as many live events (or watch recordings of live events) as possible so that they fully understand the learner experience.

While technology expands our ability to disseminate learning across our organizations, it's not about the technology; it is about well designed programs that effectively meet performance objectives. By ensuring the effective use of technology in your learning environment, you will lay the groundwork for creating online programs that are as effective (dare I say more effective?) than traditional training events.

(*Note:* Technology can also present problems during the live event. For more information on how to manage technology during a live event, see Chapter 5 of *The Synchronous Trainer's Survival Guide*.)

The Role of the Online Trainer

The final critical success factor to creating effective eLearning environments is an active and participative online instructor.

The online instructor plays a vital role to ensure that the participant is successful. Whether delivering using a traditional, synchronous, asynchronous, or blended approach participants need to feel like they have developed some kind of personal rapport with the instructor. It is even more important in an online environment than the traditional approach. The online instructor acts as an anchor, reassuring participants that support, reinforcement and assessment is readily available. "Active and participative" does not mean excessively communicating with email messages and synchronous lectures. What it means is creating an environment that is participant centered and takes the focus off of the technology and the instructor and onto the content and the learners.

So, how does the online instructor weave together the critical success factors in order to create the most effective eLearning environment?

Participant Motivation

One of the dangers of online learning is that participants feel isolated, so the online instructor becomes the central human contact point—reducing the impression that the participant is learning from a computer. The more participative the instructor, the more opportunities the instructor has to maintain a high level of motivation among participants. The instructor can be "visibly" involved in many ways—he or she can offer recognition, can conduct assessments and can facilitate relationship between remote participants. Assessment was identified as a key motivator for online participants (people will learn what they will be tested on). The online instructor manages the assessment process by giving continuous feedback and encouraging people to complete assignments in a timely manner. The effective online instructor continually reinforces online participant's performance by providing rewards and recognition of achievements.

Usable Technology

Just because the technology works it does not guarantee participant success. Introducing new learning technologies, different ways of communicating, twenty-four hour access to information can be overwhelming for even technology competent learners.

The online instructor needs to manage the learner's adoption and mastery of this new skills set without it interfering with their learning the content that is the purpose of the course. To do this, the instructor needs to begin communicating with participants several weeks ahead of time and focus on getting the technology issues out of the way before participants need to focus on the new skills and knowledge. A way to do this would be to set up a communication plan which would time-release information regarding setting up the technology, getting support whenever needed (after hours, differing time zones), and providing tech-checks and orientation to the new environment.

In order for the online instructor to do this, he or she must have full mastery of all the technologies involved in the blend. The online instructor will know they have reached this level of mastery when they are able to provide detailed learner support providing technical assistance remotely and with enough detail that the learner can follow along. For example, "If you would like to put text on the whiteboard, locate the text tool—identified by the letter A on your toolbar—click on that tool once, then click once on the whiteboard, and type your message. When you are done typing, click anywhere outside the box so that the rest of the class can see what you wrote."

Opportunities to Collaborate and Interact with One Another

Earlier in this series, we discussed the importance of designing interaction that maximized collaboration between participants. The skilled instructor will encourage collaboration even when it is not in the design of the course. Maximizing the engagement and interest of the online participants is critical to the learning outcomes. The online instructor can facilitate this by encouraging participants to speak as often as possible, to give one another feedback, minimizing lecture and maximizing interaction, and by providing feedback to the participants on the results of their collaboration.

Using language appropriately can encourage collaboration online. For example, minimize the use of techno-jargon in order to emphasize the learning and minimize the focus on technology. For example, instead of saying, "Please wait while I launch application sharing," ask participants to participate in a chat activity while you launch the application. Like magic—even a new online instructor can have an application "shared" and ready to demonstrate. Another language tip is to constantly use people's names and to circle-back to comments made earlier in the program in order to facilitate interest amongst the learners.

The Program Blend

There is a tendency to treat the individual portions of a blend (synchronous events, discussions, tutorials), as independent of one another. The active and participative instructor constantly reinforces the connections and finds ways to communicate to the participants that the asynchronous components are critical to one's overall success in the program. By ensuring that self directed work is completed in a timely manner, incorporating the knowledge gained in the self-directed portion of the course with the live-portion of the course, and continually communicating with participants throughout the blend—not just during the live events—learning becomes a continual process not a compartmentalized event.

Divide and Conquer

So you might be wondering: How an instructor successfully accomplishes all of these things while managing multiple sessions, or courses, simultaneously? The answer is a team teaching approach. Using a "producer"—known in some organizations as an assistant instructor—the instructor can focus on content and maximizing interaction, while the producer can focus on such thing as technical support, distribution of materials and emails, and validation that deadlines are being met. During the live sessions, the producer can assist by managing chat, preparing application sharing and breakout room exercises, and generally assisting the instructor with content. In essence, the course has two equally important people ensuring its success and supporting one another. To alleviate confusion, make sure that participants are aware of the dual roles, what the responsibilities of each of those people will be, and how they should direct their questions (for example, instructional or assignment questions go to the instructor; questions of a technical nature go to the producer).

Some organizations are resistant to the team teaching approach primarily because it is viewed as an additional overhead expense. The producer role does not need to be an expensive resource. Organizations have successfully used college interns, administrative assistants, and training coordinators to take on this role. In addition, an instructor can as a producer when an SME is the person responsible for delivering the content. In addition, the role of producer can fill your trainer "pipeline" by developing in-house expertise in the eLearning arena.

In order for the quality and learning outcomes of your blended solution to meet the same standards as your traditional training, use a producer to manage the administrative and technical portion of your blend.

(*Note:* For more information on the role of the online trainer, see Chapter 2 of *The Synchronous Trainer's Survival Guide*.)

Bringing It All Together

Creating a successful online learning program means more than using the latest gizmos. It means more than applying successful instructional design techniques. One needs to create a solid environment in which participants can learn. To do that we must incorporate the success factors critical to creating that environment.

Once a successful learning environment has been established, the next step is to think about the level of collaboration that is appropriate for the program and to take steps to ensure the right design has been implemented to guarantee that collaboration.

3

An Overview of Synchronous Collaboration

One of the primary selling points of synchronous classroom tools is the ability to create effective online collaboration. The sales pitch seems to make sense. When participants learn together in a traditional classroom, they have the opportunity to directly interact with one another and with the trainer. Concerns about moving courses online often seem to be related to the anticipated loss of this peer-to-peer interaction. So if online classrooms can encourage and replicate these interactions, they become more acceptable as a delivery medium and meeting space.

Characteristics of Online Collaboration

So what is online collaboration, exactly? While everyone seems to agree that it is a good idea, no one seems to be able to define the concept succinctly. As usual, to find the answer I turned to the Google™ search engine at www.google.com. Expecting to be overloaded with results, I confidently typed the term "Online Collaboration."

The "hit list" was surprisingly unsatisfying. Many of the resulting websites were vendor sites selling online collaboration tools. I had difficulty nailing down a definition. Often, the vendors said that they offered online collaboration solutions, but never went so far as to define what they meant by the term. The various software providers either thought the concept was self-evident or they did not actually have a working definition. So I focused my search a little bit and typed "Define Online Collaboration."

This produced more valuable results. Instead of vendor sites, I received articles and journals that actually discussed and attempted to define the process.

While there didn't seem to be a universally accepted definition of the concept, certain themes were obvious, such as:

- Don't confuse "collaboration" with "communication." Having access to and using tools like chat rooms, whiteboards, and application sharing does not guarantee a collaborative interaction (Kontzer, 2003).
- Do provide participants with achievable and well-defined outcomes and deliverables and guidelines or a specific process to help them achieve those outcomes. If participants do not understand what they are supposed to accomplish or how they are supposed to do it, the time will be spent on activities that do not necessarily support the goal.
- Don't encourage lecture. Design interactions that transition the trainer from "lecturer" to "facilitator."
- Do allow the participants to assist one another in the learning process. After completing independent work in an asynchronous format, participants can "collaborate" during the synchronous event to solve problems, answer questions, and pose solutions (see www.cvm.tamu.edu/wklemm/cl2.html for more information).
- Do recognize, and reward, the results of online collaboration so that participants feel as if they have engaged in a worthwhile endeavor. This will make them more responsive to future collaboration efforts.

These characteristics work together to support the ultimate goal of online collaboration, which can be summarized as follows:

> When collaborating online, using asynchronous and synchronous online tools, participant groups should be able to get results (solve problems, create project plans, design projects, and so on) that are better than the results they would have obtained working individually.

It is interesting to note that the components of online collaboration have little to do with the tools and everything to do with the people using the tools. In short, collaboration is a *human* interaction no matter how it is achieved.

Remember that simply asking individuals to work together does not result in collaboration. According to Winer and Ray (1994), there are three distinct ways in which grouped individuals can interact, *cooperation*, *coordination*, and *collaboration*:

- When individuals are *cooperating,* each individual works independently toward achieving personal objectives. Individuals will assist others when asked but they are not motivated to do so because they do not see what they have personally to gain. Asynchronous exercises should be designed to be cooperative in nature. Encourage participants to ask for assistance from the trainer or other participants using tools like email and discussion boards.
- When individuals start to regularly plan and communicate, they are involved in *coordination.* Individuals are still concerned with their personal goals, but they are willing to make allowances for group needs. The group receives the benefit of the work of each individual, but the group members still have their own personal objectives. Problems occur when an individual starts to perceive that his or her personal goal is being overshadowed by that of the group. Coordination is often the most appropriate level of collaboration in the synchronous environment. Exercises should encourage participants to work together to solve problems, while at the same time providing opportunities that ensure that each individual can master concepts on his or her own in case one or two group members choose not to collaborate fully. These can include independent exercises in workbooks, tests and assessments, and individual practice opportunities.
- When individuals put aside personal agendas in favor of the common goal of the group, they are *collaborating.* The groups create a plan to meet a goal, determine team leadership and responsibilities, and truly share resources. Successful attainment of the common goal is the ultimate achievement. This is a very altruistic outcome, and one not necessary to obtain in all learning events. True collaborative exercises are often most appropriate for goals like team building and real-life problem solving (for example, "How do we decrease our expenses by 28 percent in the next six months?"). Before you decide to include this level of collaboration, makes sure it supports your overall learning goals.

Preparing for Collaboration

Effective online collaboration generally is not a spontaneous occurrence. Unfortunately, inviting a group of participants and a trainer to the same virtual space does not guarantee that collaboration takes place in the same way that a group of people working on the same project does not constitute a team. Working together to achieve results requires planning and preparation in several areas. The trainer must be ready to facilitate, the participant must understand how to contribute, and the exercises must be well-planned and have achievable outcomes.

Preparing to Train

Organizations often assume that an effective stand-up trainer can easily transition to the synchronous environment. However, the competencies required to be an online trainer are unique in several ways.

When online, trainers need to be able to manage and interact with participants who are geographically dispersed. They must learn how to read participants' cues without the benefit of eye contact or body language. When technology fails, online trainers must be ready and able to gracefully manage the issues while trying to maintain participants' confidence in the learning environment.

Trainers new to the online environment should seek out and take advantage of every available opportunity to be a participant in synchronous programs. While observing more experienced (at least theoretically!) trainers, pay attention to how well exercises work. Take notes on what you consider

FIGURE 3.1 Online Trainer.

best practices and situations to avoid. Then, after you understand the participant experience, make sure you master the use of the collaboration tools available in your platform. The best-designed program can fail if the trainer isn't certain of how to use all of the tools.

When preparing to deliver a specific program, the trainer should rehearse, utilizing the designer and any assistant trainers in the process. This will allow the designer to answer questions about exercises and provide an opportunity for the designer to make any last-minute edits to exercise construction.

(*Note:* For more information on the role of the online trainer, see Chapter 2 of *The Synchronous Trainer's Survival Guide*.)

Preparing to Participate

Participants share the responsibility for a successful online program. Learning in this environment often requires more attention and active participation than in the traditional environment. Organizations should provide opportunities for participants to be oriented to the environment and learn the technology. Before attending the events, participants have to make the time to thoroughly complete any prework assignments to ensure that they are able to fully participate in the live session. While attending the event,

FIGURE 3.2 Student Working Online.

participants should be prepared to actively participate (not just listen!) and adhere to ground rules. (See the example in Figure 3.3.)

(*Note:* For more information on ground rules and managing online participants, see Chapter 6 of *The Synchronous Trainer's Survival Guide*.)

Only when the participants are ready and willing to exploit the online classroom can true collaboration occur.

Ground Rules

a. Turn off email and phones and clear other distractions away from your training area.
b. Participate and prepare to be called on by name.
c. Raise your if you have an immediate question or comment.
d. Be patient waiting for a response to your chat messages.
e. If you leave the program, please send a chat to the trainer when you leave and when you return.

FIGURE 3.3 Sample Ground Rules

Note: These are sample ground rules only. Each program and/or audience may have a need for a specific set of participation guidelines.

Creating Collaboration Using Online Tools

The online environment provides many ways for participants to collaborate. The asynchronous environment provides email, discussion boards, shared workspaces, and peer-to-peer networks. These types of tools allow users to create and post information, review and process information shared by others, and give each other feedback. All of this is done at the convenience of the individual, presumably managed by a training plan containing deliverables, expectations, and deadlines.

The synchronous environment provides tools for real-time collaboration, such as whiteboards, application sharing, and chat, among others. Chapters 4 through 9 examine these collaboration tools in detail in order to assist the synchronous designer in creating collaborative exercises.

Don't confuse "feedback" with interaction and collaboration. While a trainer can get valuable information from polling and other feedback mechanisms, the act of sending feedback does not in itself create collaboration.

The Value of Concurrent Participation

In order to encourage collaboration, opportunities must be provided for people to work together. When working with groups of ten, twenty, or more participants, achieving true collaboration becomes more difficult. Participation tends to be serial in nature. (For example, John talks, then Sarah talks, then Mary talks.) Generally, a trainer wouldn't ask fifteen people in a row to answer the same question verbally. There are several reasons for this:

- It would take too much time. If twenty people talk for thirty seconds each, that is ten minutes—a substantial percentage of time if the class is only one or two hours long.
- Once the first person has finished speaking, there is little incentive for that person to remain engaged for the rest of the discussion. He knows that he will not be "needed" for another nine minutes.
- It can become boring for everyone, and later participants will often respond with statements like, "I agree with everything that's been said up to this point."

For these reasons, serial exercises that include everyone in a large group are rare. I think that online collaboration should include the "voice" of all participants by

- Designing exercises for participants to work together in small groups, and
- Designing exercises that allow all of the participants in the class to participate concurrently as a large group.

If these types of exercises are not included, some participants will be frustrated because their opinions were not heard, while others will see the opportunity to opt out of exercises and accomplish personal tasks—while keeping one "ear" to the classroom in case the trainer tries to engage them. Another risk is that the program will tend to be more lecture-oriented because the onus will be on the trainer to keep the course moving forward.

Creating concurrent collaborative exercises, during which all of the participants are working at the same time, minimizes lecture and increases the opportunity for participants to learn from one another in addition to learning from the trainer. Several versatile tools support concurrent collaboration:

- The breakout room tool is a very effective way to facilitate small-group work. Participants can be divided up and encouraged to collaborate. Each group works independently. At the end of the exercise the groups can be recalled to the main classroom to discuss the results of their collaboration. (Examples are provided in Chapter 6.)
- A group chat room allows everyone to communicate with everyone else simultaneously using text. (Examples are provided in Chapter 5.) When the group becomes very large, the trainer may need assistance with facilitation, but this type of application can accommodate a group of almost any size.
- A multi-user whiteboard allows, at the discretion of the trainer, everyone to write on whiteboard slides at the same time. (Examples are provided in Chapter 4.) With planning, this type of exercise can accommodate up to twenty participants successfully.

Remember, these tool variations are not available in all synchronous platforms. For example, some vendors have determined that an "instant messaging" approach is more appropriate than a group chat area. (Check www.insynctraining.com and click on resources for information on what tools are provided by individual software vendors.)

I recently had a discussion with a representative from a vendor that did not provide a full multi-user whiteboard. When I explained why I thought it was such a powerful tool and why I thought it should be included with their platform, the representative responded that those exercises would be too difficult to facilitate. My response was, "Get a better class of facilitator! Don't limit ME!" In fact, these types of activities can be easily facilitated and highly successful if the exercise is well-planned and the trainer has a chance to practice. Chapter 4 provides detailed examples of successful whiteboard exercises.

Designing Exercises

Now that the program design, learning environment, and collaboration level have been considered, the next step is to create collaborative synchronous exercises. When used effectively, synchronous tools like audio, whiteboards, chat, breakout rooms, application sharing, and synchronous web browsing can support the learning design and program collaboration goals.

4

Whiteboard Exercises and Techniques

Some variation of the whiteboard tool is found in virtually every synchronous classroom platform. Roughly the synchronous equivalent of a traditional flip chart, whiteboards allow trainers and participants to post ideas on a shared space. Images and content can be placed on prepared whiteboards (often in the form of PowerPoint slides) and then marked up ("annotated") using a variety of drawing tools.

It's a mistake to think of the whiteboard simply as a flip chart, however. That is truly minimizing the potential of the tool. When thoughtfully designed, whiteboard exercises can be truly interactive and collaborative.

Collaborative whiteboard exercises can make the program seem to move more quickly for participants and can help to minimize lecture. They are also great for engaging kinesthetic learners (people who take in information by being physically engaged with some task).

Instructional Uses

Here are some basic ideas to help the instructional designer create collaborative exercises using the whiteboard. (See Figure 4.1.) More detailed examples are provided at the end of this chapter.

- You can use the whiteboard for anything you would use a flip chart or marker board for in a traditional classroom setting. For example, you can capture expectations at the beginning of a class and revisit them at the end of a program.
- Content changes and additions can be captured and used to revise the program. In many programs, participants or trainers make pertinent points that should be captured for future scripts or slides. If these ideas

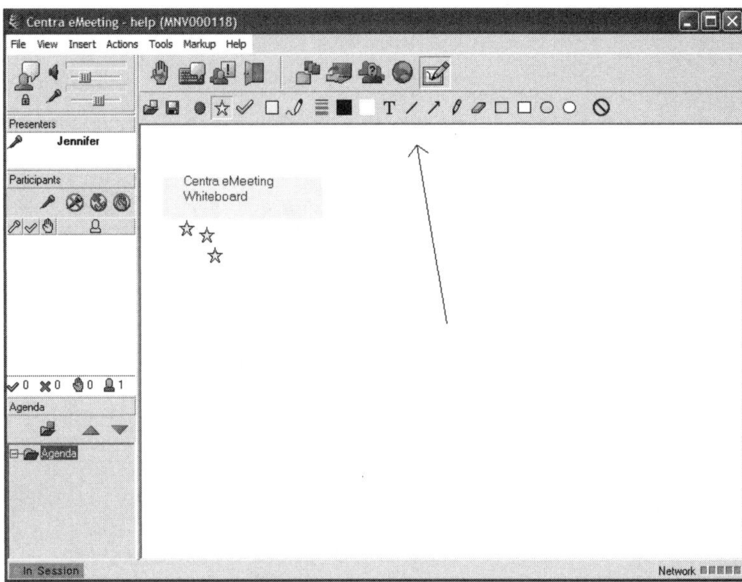

FIGURE 4.1 Whiteboard File.

are captured on the whiteboard, the recordings can be reviewed later on and the new ideas can be incorporated.

- You can capture participants' ideas flip-chart style. Design screens with minimal text (two or three words or perhaps just a graphic) and a white background. Engage the participants in a discussion and capture their ideas on the whiteboard.
- Whiteboards can often be archived for reuse in asynchronous applications or emailed to class participants. Participants often want to receive a copy of the results of effective whiteboard collaborations.
- Content can be highlighted as it is discussed, which makes lectures more meaningful. There are a variety of annotation tools available, so plan which ones you would like to use and how you would like to use them.
- Ask experienced participants to take turns annotating the whiteboard (that is, scribing comments they think are important) while you are moderating a discussion. Besides keeping them busy, it is interesting to see what points the participants find interesting.
- Icebreakers and games can also be created using the whiteboard. Break away from the content and start to have fun! Crossword puzzles, hangman, and Jeopardy™ games can all be very engaging and useful when trying to reinforce concepts.
- Use the whiteboard as a polling tool. Ask participants to graphically vote on which bullet point on a screen they think is most important by using a specific annotation tool (maybe a star, checkmark, or pointer).

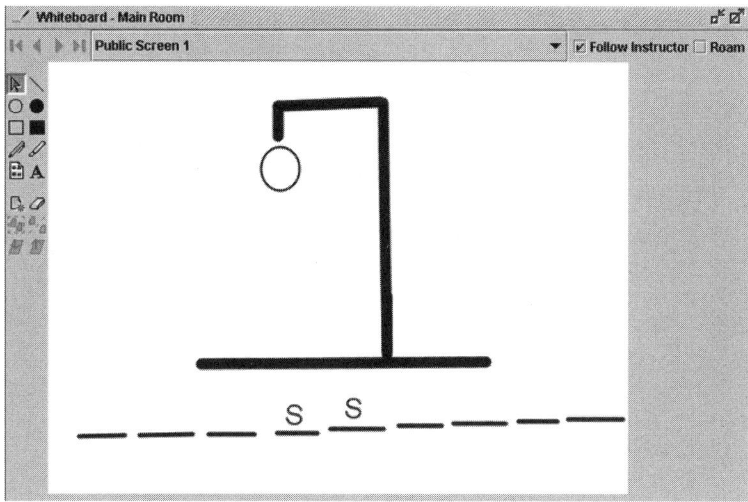

FIGURE 4.2 Sample Whiteboard Drawing.

Tool Variations and Considerations

Not all whiteboards are the same. Each product has its own variation and conceptualization of how the tool works most effectively. Before designing exercises, it is important to thoroughly understand the intricacies of the specific tool you are using. Here are some questions you should ask before designing collaborative whiteboard exercises.

- *How many people can write on the whiteboard at once?* This is probably the biggest differentiator between different whiteboard types and the characteristic that will most affect your exercise design. Some vendors feel that only the trainer should be able to write on the whiteboard. Others allow the trainer to select one participant at a time to use the tools. Still others allow potentially everyone in the class to annotate at the same time.
- *Is all uploaded content available on the whiteboard?* Sometimes you need to make a decision while assembling course content about which screens should be whiteboard screens. (I always attempt to make ALL of my screens whiteboard compatible.) Other platforms automatically make any web-ready content (PowerPoint, gifs, and jpgs) available on the whiteboard.
- *What tools are available for whiteboard drawings?* Squares, circles, pointers, stars, lines, "typed" text, and highlighters are all examples of common whiteboard tools. Some products allow users to change font and line colors. One fun feature found in a few platforms gives every participant a custom pointer tool.

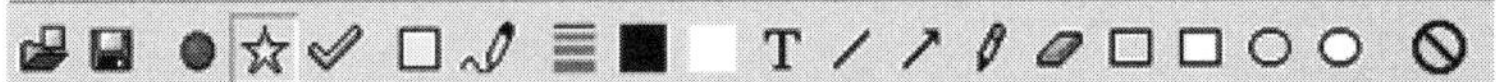

FIGURE 4.3 Centra Whiteboard Tools.

- *Can you save whiteboards created during the event?* Some trainers find it useful to save the results of collaborative whiteboard exercises and distribute them to participants or other interested parties after the event is over. The whiteboards may be saved as a common file type (.bmp, .jpg, .gif), or the vendor may have a proprietary file format that can only be used within that application. Vendors that don't support this suggest that you watch recordings to review the results.
- *Can graphics be pasted or imported to the whiteboard?* This allows for some creativity during the program. Instead of having all whiteboard slides prepared ahead of time, engaging graphics can be imported based on the current class personality. Sometimes participants may be able to import graphics as well. This can be the basis for some fun, engaging interactions, but participants must be warned to be careful about the nature of the graphical content they decide to share.
- *Is the snapshot feature available?* It can be very useful to capture a picture of an application and paste it onto the whiteboard so it can be explained in more detail.
- *If you return to a slide that you have written on, will the comments still be there?* In a traditional classroom, trainers often capture information on flip charts and return to them later in the program. Some whiteboard variations allow you to do this as well. For example, if the trainer writes on Slide #2, every time he or she returns to that slide during the program the annotations will still be there.
- *Can drawings and graphics be moved once they are placed on the whiteboard?* If they can, you have an "object-oriented" whiteboard. Being able to move or erase individual whiteboard additions can make for some interesting exercises!

Best Practices and Techniques

Keep the following tips in mind when designing and facilitating whiteboard interactions:

- Plan what drawing tools you want to use for each exercise. Give thought to colors, fonts, and shapes. Using these tools effectively will maximize the visual impact of the exercise.

- Be very clear in the instructions about who should be writing on the whiteboard and what he or she is supposed to accomplish. If you are allowing one participant at a time to write, how will that participant be selected? If multiple people are participating, how will that be facilitated?
- Implement ground rules. When providing exercise instructions, make sure participants understand the following guidelines (and add whatever additional guidelines you feel are necessary):
  - Participants should be sensitive about the content of any graphics that they import to the whiteboard.
  - The "Clear Whiteboard" tool should only be used by the trainer!
  - Don't worry about spelling mistakes, bad handwriting, or writing outside the lines. The point is to be creative.

Sample Exercises

The rest of this chapter contains five detailed examples of whiteboard exercises. PowerPoint is the graphic medium used unless otherwise indicated. Sometimes, an assistant trainer, or producer, can be very helpful in facilitating these exercises. Because of this, instructions have been included for the trainer, producer, and participants.

Before designing comparable exercises for your initiatives, make sure you consider the software variations of your specific platform and test the exercises in a realistic setting. You may need to make accommodations for your particular synchronous platform.

In general, trainer and producer (assistant trainer) instructions will be available in a leader guide. Participant instructions will be delivered by the trainer verbally and be supported by screen instructions and participant guide references when appropriate. A sample leader guide is located in Appendix E, and a sample participant guide is located in Appendix F.

At the end of each exercise, there is room for you to take notes on how you may be able to customize the interaction for your specific projects. Make sure you keep track of the new ways you find to use the tools to collaborate online.

 **Whiteboard Exercise 1**

EXPECTATIONS

Exercise Name Expectations

Type of Exercise Program Warm-Up

Required Tool Functionality Whiteboard that everyone can write on at the same time

Instructional Objective/Purpose

1. To get participants accustomed to participating by providing a low-risk exercise
2. To capture participants' thoughts about what they are going to gain from the program so they can be reviewed later
3. To ensure that the expectations of the trainer and the participants are the same

Timing Up to five minutes

Constraints This will not work well as a whiteboard exercise if there are more than twenty participants. There is probably not enough room on the screen to accomodate more participants.

Design Considerations and Exercise Set-Up

- Estimate the number of participants in the class and create a grid containing 8, 9, 12, 16, or 20 squares to match the approximate number of participants.
- If participants' names are known prior to the class, the names should be typed into the grid ahead of time in order to save time. If a list of names is not available, the grid boxes should be numbered.
- Consider the example of a new hire training program. The exercise steps might look like this:
    1. Whiteboard tools are provided to each participant.
    2. Each participant is assigned a spot on the grid.
    3. Participants are instructed to use the text or drawing tools in their assigned grid space to let the trainer know at least one expectation of this program. To encourage creativity, text or illustrations are acceptable.

4. Participants should indicate they have completed the exercise by clicking "Yes."
5. After about two minutes, the trainer should debrief the expectations exercise by asking a few participants to explain their responses in depth.

EXPECTATIONS				
1	2	3	4	5
6	7	8	9	10
11	12	13	14	15
16	17	18	19	20

Trainer Instructions

- If using numbers in the grid, the participants need to be assigned spaces. If your synchronous platform assigns numbers to participants when they raise their hands, ask everyone to raise his or her hand and leave it raised. Tell them that the number next to their names corresponds to the numbers in the grid. Ask participants to click "Yes" or "OK" to verify that they know where they need to write. (Another way to assign spaces is to have the producer type a set of participant initials in each grid box as the trainer verbally assigns each space.)
- Ensure that everyone is given permission to write on the whiteboard.
- Give participants one minute to capture their thoughts about what they expect to accomplish during this session.
- Take two to four minutes to debrief the exercise, indicating which expectations should be met during the program. (Make the debriefing fun by commenting on illustrations, use of color, and so forth.)
- Save the whiteboard results so you can review them at the end of the program.
- At the end of the program, take several minutes to verify that you met the expectations.

Producer Instructions

The producer can assist by:

- Typing participants' names in the grid if there is no other way to assign numbers.
- Assigning whiteboard permissions.
- Saving the whiteboard at the end of the exercise or taking notes on the participants' expectations.
- Assisting participants with whiteboard tools.

Participant Instructions

Directions to participants should be concise and easy to understand. Verbally instruct participants on what they will be doing. Consider including exercise instructions in the participant guide.

- Using the whiteboard tools, communicate your expectations on the grid. You may type text or create a drawing illustrating your expectations.
- When you are finished, use any remaining time to review the expectations of your peers.

Exercise Notes and Variations

- Ask three participants to select someone else's annotation and explain what it means to the rest of the class.
- This same type of exercise can be accomplished using a group chat area.
- More than twenty boxes in a grid becomes too much. Consider using chat or a combination of chat and whiteboard techniques.

How can YOU use this exercise, or a variation, in your program?

 Whiteboard Exercise 2

MAKING CONNECTIONS

Exercise Name	Making Connections
Type of Exercise	Instructional game to promote creative thinking; use as a warm-up or icebreaker
Required Tool Functionality	Whiteboard
Instructional Objective/Purpose	To allow participants to connect two or more concepts and see the interrelationship between seemingly unrelated items
Timing	Up to five minutes

Design Considerations and Exercise Set-Up

- The screen should contain between six and twelve phrases, numbers, or pictures. There should be some obvious relationships, and some less obvious relationships, among the items.
- Consider the example of an underwriting claims training program. The exercise steps might look like this:
  1. Participants are presented with a screen containing pictures of the following items: a bicycle, a volcano, a jewelry pendant, a construction worker, a person working at a computer, and a house with a family standing in front of it.
  2. Ask for up to three volunteers to use the whiteboard line tool to connect two items and then explain the connection. They may or may not be related to content. For example: A person may ride a bicycle on a volcano path or the person working at the computer may be processing a claim for volcano damages.
  3. Ask for up to three more volunteers to use the whiteboard tools to connect three or four items and then explain the connection. For example: The people in front of the house may be filing a claim with the underwriter sitting at the computer for a lost pendant or the construction worker may be fixing the home that was damaged after a recent volcano.

Making Connections

Trainer Instructions

- Explain to the class that the screen contains up to twelve concepts and illustrations that have various relationships to one another. Some items may have multiple relationships. Phrases may be connected to other phrases or to illustrations. For example, a picture of an apple might be related to the word "fruit" and the word "red" and a picture of a "pie."
- In series, ask participants to select an item or phrase and connect that item to as many other items as possible. They will be asked to explain the connections verbally, while the trainer draws lines connecting the items and indicates with text what those connections were.
- After the first participant is done, the trainer clears the whiteboard annotations to prepare for the next participant, who selects a different starting point and makes as many connections as he or she can. Duplicates are OK, as long as the starting point is different.

Note: If you have more participants than you need to complete this exercise, make a note to include the extra participants first in the next exercise.

- Debrief using a "Seven Degrees of Separation" technique. Say, "We've identified a lot of different relationships here. Let me show you how these two seemingly unrelated items are connected. Then use four or more steps to connect them. For example: The word 'RED'> a picture of an 'APPLE'> a picture of a 'PIE'> a picture of a 'CIRCLE' (Think about the word 'PI'—We tricked you!). Hence, we connected RED to CIRCLE."

Producer Instructions

The producer can assist by:

- Drawing lines and typing connections on the whiteboard.
- Keeping track of how many connections were identified by each participant.

Participant Instructions

Directions to participants should be concise and easy to understand. Verbally instruct participants on what they will be doing. Consider including exercise instructions in the participant guide.

- Be creative! As long as you can support your connection, and the class buys in, it counts.

Exercise Notes and Variations

- Make this into a contest. The participant who makes the most connections from a single starting point wins!
- Turn the idea around. Ask participants to come up with ways seemingly unrelated items might be related. The first one to come up with the connection in the fewest number of steps wins.
- Ask a participant to add another item to the whiteboard and encourage the rest of the class to try to make additional connections.

How can YOU use this exercise, or a variation, in your program?

 Whiteboard Exercise 3

DATA ENTRY

Exercise Name	Data Entry
Type of Exercise	Discovery/Software Instruction
Required Tool Functionality	Whiteboard
Instructional Objective/Purpose	To instruct participants about how to complete transactions and/or enter data into an application
Outcomes	Participants will be able to coach one another about how to complete a screen in an application.
Timing	Ten to fifteen minutes

Design Considerations and Exercise Set-Up

- Have a series of application screens (for example, three data-entry screens required to input a new customer into the system) pasted onto whiteboard slides ahead of time.
- Create a short scenario for each screen. These scenarios should contain information necessary to complete the screen, but not in any logical order. Some information may be buried or not provided. The scenarios, when brought together, should complete an entire larger transaction.
- Include these scenarios along with the screen shots in the participant guide.
- Consider the example of a training program that teaches how to enroll a new customer into the system. The exercise steps might look like this:
  1. Screen one requires customer demographic data. Using the whiteboard tools, circle a field on the screen. Ask a participant to review the scenario and tell you what specific data from that scenario should be in that field. "Type" the answer into the field using the whiteboard text tools.
  2. Circle another field and ask a different participant to use the whiteboard tools to type the correct data, based on the scenario, into the field.
  3. Repeat as appropriate, then move to the next screen.

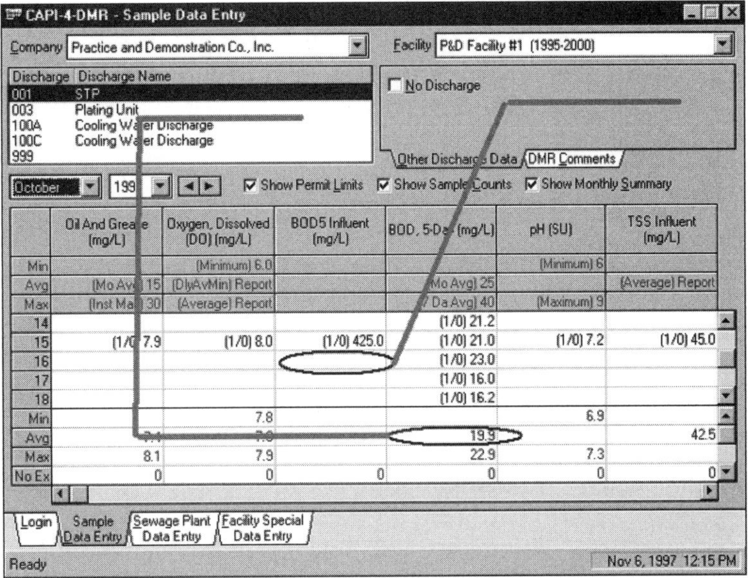

Trainer Instructions

- Assign each participant one of the participant guide scenarios. (For larger classes you may need to assign two participants per scenario. Not everyone may be able to participate.)
- Ask for a volunteer to use the whiteboard tools to fill in the screen capture using the information provided in the scenario. Remember to assign whiteboard permissions as necessary.
- Follow up by asking the participant what he or she thinks will happen next in the transaction.

Producer Instructions

The producer can assist by:

- Having the application ready to launch in case participants need additional demonstrations.
- Grabbing "snapshots" of screens for additional exercises.

Participant Instructions

Directions to participants should be concise and easy to understand. Verbally instruct participants on what they will be doing. Consider including exercise instructions in the participant guide.

- Write down questions about the scenario as you review it.
- Ask other participants why they made certain decisions.

Exercise Notes and Variations

- If participants reach mastery faster than expected, "snapshot" additional screen captures and paste them onto the whiteboard and do an advanced round. Participants can provide each other with data to complete the screens.
- If participants have trouble with a particular concept, follow up the exercise with an application sharing demonstration.
- For a more advanced group, consider creating a breakout room exercise for two participants that brings them through a series of screens.

How can YOU use this exercise, or a variation, in your program?

Whiteboard Exercise 4

APPLYING THE PROCESS

Exercise Name	Applying the Process
Type of Exercise	Independent Work Review/Problem Solving
Required Tool Functionality	Whiteboard
Instructional Objective/Purpose	1. To ensure that participants have completed and understood independent work exercises 2. To have the class collaborate to help an individual solve a problem in class
Outcomes	Participants will collaborate to solve a problem using a process reviewed during a prework assignment
Timing	Five to ten minutes

Design Considerations and Exercise Set-Up

- Participants need to complete a prework assignment that informs them of a process, for example, how to deal with difficult employees.
- Participants should complete a short questionnaire around the topic prior to class, for example: "Think of a difficult employee . . .
  - What characteristics make you classify him or her as difficult?
  - What have you done to fix the problem?
  - How did he or she respond?
  - How does his or her behavior affect the people around you?
- Have participants send the answers to these questions to the trainer before the class begins.
- Create a slide that contains the sample questions and room for one set of responses.

Applying The Process
Think of a difficult employee...
? What characteristics make you classify him or her as difficult?
? What have you done to fix the problem?
? How did he or she respond?
? How does his or her behavior affect the people around you?"

Trainer Instructions

- Pick a participant at random and have him or her write responses to the prework questions on the whiteboard.
- Ask participants to help solve this person's problem by applying the process learned during prework. They should think about the process and apply it to the specifics presented by the randomly selected participant. The focus at this point is on the process, not on each participant's prework.
- When the class is finished, debrief the exercise by going through the formal process and applying it to the presented problem. Comment on how well (or not) the participants applied the process.

Producer Instructions

- Capture participants' suggestions on the whiteboard.

Participant Instructions

Directions to participants should be concise and easy to understand. Verbally instruct participants on what they will be doing. Consider including exercise instructions in the participant guide.

- Make sure you complete all prework and the questionnaire.

Exercise Notes and Variations

- Ask participants who do not submit prework responses ahead of time to attend a different session.

How can YOU use this exercise, or a variation, in your program?

Whiteboard Exercise 5

GET OUT THE VOTE

Exercise Name	Get Out the Vote
Type of Exercise	Icebreaker
Required Tool Functionality	Whiteboard that everyone can write on at the same time
Instructional Objective/Purpose	To obtain opinions or group consensus
Outcomes	Everyone in the class will be able to see a group consensus
Timing	Two minutes

Design Considerations and Exercise Set-Up

- A question and a series of response options are recorded on a slide for the audience. For example: "Of the following meals, which do you think is most important?"

  a. Breakfast

  b. Lunch

  c. Dinner

Get Out The VOTE!!!!!!
Of the following meals, which do YOU think is the most important?
• Breakfast ☆☆☆☆☆☆☆☆
• Lunch
• Dinner ☆☆

Trainer Instructions

- Grant everyone whiteboard permission and ask participants to indicate their choice using a graphical representation. Some platforms offer stars, check marks, or pointers.
- Some participants may feel so strongly about one choice that they "vote" several times. Or if they are split between choices, they may vote for multiple choices. This should be encouraged. The idea of this exercise is to give the group a visual of which choice is the most important to them. Exuberance adds to the experience.

Participant Instructions

Directions to participants should be concise and easy to understand. Verbally instruct participants on what they will be doing. Consider including exercise instructions in the participant guide.

- Use the whiteboard tools to vote for your choice. If you feel strongly, let the group know! This is not a "one man, one vote" situation.

Exercise Notes and Variations

- This can be more visually effective than polling because the trainer can annotate the votes, for example, by drawing a circle around the most popular selection and a square around the least popular selection. The trainer may ask a question such as, "Why do you think choice #1 received the most votes?" The trainer can capture those opinions on the whiteboard to add emphasis to the voting results.

How can YOU use this exercise, or a variation, in your program?

5

Chat Exercises and Techniques

Text-based chat allows the participants and trainer to communicate with one another through text messaging. Some version of chat is included in every synchronous classroom. It is most commonly used to ask questions or request technical assistance. While these are very valuable functions, there is so much more that can be done with this tool.

A public group chat room allows all of the participants to post and review each other's messages. Private messaging allows participants to signal difficulties without disrupting a session. It may also allow participants to privately communicate with one another. Often, chat discussions (or transcripts) can be saved as text files and used after the event is over. An example is shown in Figure 5.1.

Like the whiteboard, collaborative chat exercises engage those kinesthetic learners who need to stay active. It also is an attractive communication method for those who take in information best by reading and communicate their ideas best by writing. Using chat ensures that everyone can have his or her opinion heard by at least the trainer, if not everyone in the classroom.

Trainers are often concerned about the ability for participants to have text-based conversations during a lecture or exercise, whether or not the conversations are related to the content. It is potentially distracting to the trainer and other participants and can indicate that the participants are not paying attention. Besides, it just seems so rude! My philosophy is different. I encourage full use of the chat for several reasons:

- I understand that some people need to be physically engaged in something to stay focused on listening. (I am one of those people!) By allowing these participants to type and send out chat messages, you are actually encouraging them to stay engaged.

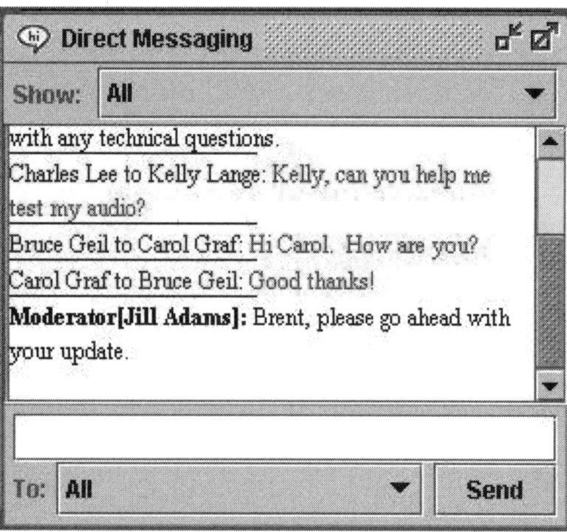

FIGURE 5.1 vClass Full Group Chat.

- If participants are chatting about content-related ideas, it can provide clues to the trainer. If they are asking questions of one another, perhaps the content is being presented at a level that is too high for some members of the audience. If they are discussing the content in depth, maybe you have some experts you can use to assist with the class. (Every time you can change the voice of the speaker, you create an opportunity to re-engage participants who may have mentally drifted away.)
- When the trainer notices a sudden sharp increase in text communication, it is probably a good time to wrap up his or her thoughts, take a break, and review the information. One of two things has probably occurred. The participants have hit a point where they can't take in more information (and a break might be necessary) or some concept requires more explanation. Without body language and eye contact, a flurry of activity (or for that matter, a total LACK of activity) is an important cue.

Don't worry too much about the overuse of the chat for non-instructional purposes. Most participants behave. And if it becomes too difficult to facilitate, the trainer may be able to turn off the feature.

Instructional Uses

Here are some basic ideas to help the instructional designer create collaborative exercises using chat. More detailed examples are provided at the end of this chapter.

- It seems that there are certain participants who become more open with each perceived level of anonymity. Participants who are more reserved and who may not feel comfortable expressing themselves verbally are often more likely to interact when text chat options are available. You may find that some groups prefer text chat.
- Use this tool as a re-engagement technique. No matter how many people are speaking, it can be difficult to listen actively for long periods of time. This is especially true for participants for whom listening is not a preferred intake style. By moving the interactions to the chat area, you can break up delivery methodologies and keep more participants engaged throughout the program.
- Use the chat area as a brainstorming area for participants to share as many ideas as possible in a short period of time. Brainstorming rules apply (see Figure 5.2)!
- If you have a technical support person online, he or she can monitor the chat to identify and fix technical problems without interrupting the class. If you happen to be using a subject-matter expert, he or she can monitor a classroom in order to answer content-related questions that may be out of the scope of the current lecture or activity.
- When designing chat exercises, you may have prewritten questions or exercise instructions that you want to use. You may be able to create a word processing document that contains these items and use copy/paste keys to transfer them to the chat area quickly. It minimizes the time it takes to conduct these exercises and ensures that all necessary information is properly communicated.
- If two participants can privately communicate, you can create effective "pairs" exercises for brainstorming, problem solving, or even competitive contests.

Brainstorming Rules

- All ideas are worthwhile, don't judge them
- Get ideas out; don't discuss them
- Record all ideas
- Expect wild ideas
- Be spontaneous – don't hold back
- Suspend judgments
- Quantity counts more than quality
- Try to build on each others' ideas

FIGURE 5.2 Brainstorming Rules.

Tool Variations and Considerations

Not all chats are the same. Each product has its own variation and conceptualization of how the tool works most effectively. Before designing exercises, it is important to thoroughly understand the intricacies of your specific tool. Here are some questions you should ask before designing collaborative chat exercises.

- *Is full group chat available?* Full group chat allows everyone to read public messages posted by everyone else. The feature allows for true concurrent collaboration, but exercises need to be well planned and facilitated to avoid chaotic situations.
- *Is "instant messaging" available?* Some platforms offer an Instant Messenger, or "Notes," type approach in addition to, or instead of, group chat. This effectively supports one-on-one collaboration, but is limited for large group exercises because only two people can communicate with each other.
- *Is private messaging to the trainer/assistant trainer available?* There are a variety of reasons that a participant may want to chat privately with a trainer, including technical problems, questions about content, and telling the trainer that he or she needs to leave the class for a while. If a participant hasn't been active for a while, the trainer may want to contact him or her to offer support.
- *Is private messaging between participants allowed?* If participants can communicate privately, you can design "pairs" exercises for small group collaboration. Some platforms allow the trainer to see all private chat messages. You may also have the option to turn off the ability for participants to privately communicate.
- *Are chat transcripts available?* Often you can get a transcript of the chat interactions in text format. These transcripts allow the trainer to review questions after the event and respond to participants in a very detailed way. It can also function as a way to keep minutes and document responsibilities. If a transcript is available, find out if it includes private messages.
- *Can chat be suspended?* You may be able to suspend group chat and/or private chat functions mid-class or when setting up the class. Find out how and when this is possible.
- *Can you paste text into the chat area?* This ability allows you to plan detailed chat exercises and quickly copy/paste (using keyboard commands, as shown in Figure 5.3) instructions and comments into the chat area while the exercise is taking place.

Keystroke	Action	Useful in:
CTRL + c	Copy	Chat area and Whiteboard
CTRL + x	Cut	Chat area and Whiteboard
CTRL + v	Paste	Chat area and Whiteboard
CTRL + z	Undo	Application sharing
CTRL + PgDn	Go to top of next page	Application sharing
CTRL + PgUp	Go to top of previous page	Application sharing
CTRL + End	Go to end of document	Application sharing
CTRL + Home	Go to beginning of document	Application sharing

FIGURE 5.3 Common Keyboard Commands.

- *Can you copy text out of the chat area and paste on the whiteboard?* This ability allows you to elaborate on a specific point or question that was introduced in the chat area. Once the comment is on the whiteboard, the trainer can facilitate a group discussion to drill deeper.

Best Practices and Techniques

Keep these tips in mind when designing and facilitating chat interactions.

- Encourage chatting. Don't worry about it being disruptive right away. Most people behave themselves. If you start noticing a problem, you can intervene at that point.
- Provide time boundaries in chat exercises. Participants want to know how much time they have to complete the written articulation of their thoughts. When time starts running out, make an announcement. ("Take fifteen seconds to complete your thoughts.")
- Be specific about anticipated outcomes. Participants need to have very clear instructions about what you expect them to accomplish. A way to support this is to create a slide that has the instructions, outcomes, and time boundaries, like the one in Figure 5.4.
- Let participants reflect on peer responses. Always make sure there is some time for participants to review each other's postings. Ask if they want to comment on a particular response. This helps to ensure that participants don't feel as if their time and ideas were wasted.

How Do You Deal With Difficult Customers?
1. Go to the chat area
2. Type in as many answers to this question as you can, each in a separate note
3. Click "OK" when you are done.
4. Take a few seconds to read the responses of other participants
1 Minute

FIGURE 5.4 Chat Instructions.

- Implement ground rules. When providing exercise instructions, make sure participants understand the following guidelines (and add whatever additional guidelines you feel are necessary!):
  - Don't worry about spelling and grammar mistakes. This is a type of brainstorming exercise.
  - The rules of brainstorming apply.
- Tell participants whether the trainer can see private chats between participants.

Sample Exercises

The rest of this chapter contains five detailed examples of chat exercises. Sometimes, an assistant trainer, or producer, can be very helpful in facilitating these exercises. Because of this, instructions have been included for the trainer, producer, and participants.

Before designing comparable exercises for your own initiatives, make sure you consider the software variations of your specific platform and test the exercises in a realistic setting. You may need to make accommodations for your particular synchronous platform.

In general, trainer and producer (assistant trainer) instructions will be available in a leader guide. Participant instructions will be delivered verbally by the trainer and be supported by screen instructions and participant guide references when appropriate. A sample leader guide is located in Appendix E, and a sample participant guide is located in Appendix F.

At the end of each exercise there is room for you to take notes on how you may be able to customize the interaction for your specific projects. Make sure you keep track of the new ways you find to use the tools to collaborate online.

Chat Exercise 1

LET'S TALK ABOUT FEEDBACK

Exercise Name	Let's Talk About Feedback
Type of Exercise	Discussion and Feedback
Required Tool Functionality	Group chat (everyone can type at once) Chat archiving
Instructional Objective/Purpose	To provide an individual real-time feedback that can be referred to after the synchronous event
Timing	Varies

Design Considerations and Exercise Set-Up

- Participants should all prepare materials (speech, solution to an assigned problem, problem description, opinion, and such items) intended to be presented to the group. This should be completed prior to the live event.
- A list of requirements (required elements, timing, interactions, and so forth) for the presentation and activity should be included in the participant guide.
- The participant guide should also contain a feedback list for the participants to use to evaluate the presentation.
- To confirm that this independent work is completed, participants should send their scenario to the trainer prior to the live event.
- Consider the example of a customer service training program. The exercise steps might look like this:
  1. Prior to the live event, participants were asked to come up with up to three ways to deal with an irate and abusive customer and to prepare a one-minute discussion on these techniques.
  2. During the live event, the trainer selects a participant at random and asks that he or she explain his or her response while all participants provide feedback about the effectiveness of the proposed techniques using the chat area.

Trainer Instructions

- This exercise can occur in the large group or in breakout rooms.
- This can be used as a warm-up exercise where only one or two people need to take a turn in the full classroom or as a major exercise where everyone has a turn in breakout rooms of three people each.
- Take the first turn to provide a model for the participants.
- Don't ask for volunteers; select participants at random. You don't want to teach people that they don't need to complete independent work as long as they don't volunteer to present it.
- Launch a blank whiteboard or supporting slide for the participant who is presenting.
- Support the presenter by scribing on the whiteboard during the presentation.
- At the end of the presentation, give participants an extra minute or so to finish writing their comments in the text chat area.
- Save the text chat with the participant's name and move on to the next participant.

Producer Instructions

The producer can assist by:

- Scribing on the whiteboard for the presenting participant. This leaves the trainer free to provide feedback.
- Saving the text chat at the end of each presentation.
- Compiling and arranging feedback comments.
- Setting up breakout rooms, if applicable.

Participant Instructions

Directions to participants should be concise and easy to understand. Verbally instruct participants on what they will be doing. Consider including exercise instructions in the participant guide.

- As the selected participant is giving the presentation, send specific feedback via chat using the feedback list in your participant guide as an example.
- This is not a conversation. Chat comments are directed toward the presenter only.

Exercise Notes and Variations

- If this is a multiple event program, the trainer should model the expected deliverables at the end of one session so that participants can complete prework.
- Tell participants that if they give their scenarios to the trainer a full two days before the live event they can also send one PowerPoint slide to support the presentation. The trainer has to sequence this slide into the course materials or into breakout room content, depending on how the exercise is being facilitated.

How can YOU use this exercise, or a variation, in your program?

Chat Exercise 2

BRAINSTORMING AND GROUP COLLABORATION

Exercise Name	Brainstorming and Group Collaboration
Type of Exercise	Brainstorming
Required Tool Functionality	Group chat (everyone can type at once)
Instructional Objective/Purpose	1. To capture as many ideas as possible about a series of topics in a short period of time 2. To encourage creative thinking.
Timing	Five minutes

Design Considerations and Exercise Set-Up

- Create a whiteboard slide with up to three questions, related or unrelated. An example might be "What do you need to do to make sure you meet a very tight deadline?" Leave room to type ideas under each question.
- The whiteboard may also contain a small graphic with the rules of brainstorming represented.

Trainer Instructions

- Explain that participants should answer each question with as many responses as possible. Each answer should be on a separate text line in the chat area.

Brainstorming
• What do you need to make sure you meet a very tight deadline?
• What barriers are usually in your way?

Brainstorming Rules
• All ideas are worthwhile, don't judge them • Get ideas out; don't discuss them • Record all ideas • Expect wild ideas • Be spontaneous – don't hold back • Suspend judgments • Quantity counts more than quality • Try to build on each others' ideas

FIGURE 5.5 Sample Exercise.

- Tell participants that the rules of brainstorming apply.
- Each brainstorming session should last forty-five to sixty seconds.
- At the end of one session, read the next question and start immediately again.
- At the end of the questions, take a five-minute class break or assign an exercise in the participant guide while you review the results and prepare to debrief the exercise.
- Type the most common ideas under the questions on the slide using the annotation tools.
- Debrief by congratulating the participants on their creativity and highlighting common answer themes.

Producer Instructions

- Assist with compiling results.

Participant Instructions

Directions to participants should be concise and easy to understand. Verbally instruct participants on what they will be doing. Consider including exercise instructions in the participant guide.

- Be as creative as possible and share as many ideas as possible.

Exercise Notes and Variations

- Brainstorming can be used as a lead-in to another exercise. Use just one question and use participants' responses to introduce a new concept or a new process.

How can YOU use this exercise, or a variation, in your program?

Chat Exercise 3

LET'S PAIR UP!

Exercise Name	Let's Pair Up!
Type of Exercise	Pairs Collaboration
Required Tool Functionality	Private chat between individual participants
Instructional Objective/Purpose	1. To allow pairs of participants to privately collaborate to solve a problem related to the content 2. To give participants the experience of being thrown together on a collaborative team with vague objectives with unknown outcomes
Timing	Two minutes per collaboration

Design Considerations and Exercise Set-Up

- Create a whiteboard containing a problem related to the content, for example, "Based on the scenario you just watched via streaming video, what do you suggest that Veronica do next?"

Trainer Instructions

- Identify the participants who will be working with one another.
- Remind participants how to use private chat.
- Explain that the purpose of this exercise is to discuss the question on the whiteboard.
- Debrief by asking several groups to answer the question or identify the item. Stop when this starts to become redundant.

Let's Pair Up!
Based on the scenario you just saw, what would you expect Veronica to do next? • Discuss with your partner using private chat. • Come to consensus about next steps. **2 minutes**

FIGURE 5.6 Sample Exercise.

- Continue the debriefing by asking questions about the interactions: Did one participant take charge? Was it difficult to work together? What would have made collaboration easier?

Producer Instructions

The producer can assist by:

- Typing the names of the people paired up on the whiteboard.

Participant Instructions

Directions to participants should be concise and easy to understand. Verbally instruct participants on what they will be doing. Consider including exercise instructions in the participant guide.

- Work together to solve a problem in a short period of time using only text to communicate.
- Be ready to report back on your answers.

Exercise Notes and Variations

- Place a series of questions on the whiteboard and assign a different question to each group.
- Instead of a question, place an unusual graphic on the whiteboard and ask the pairs to come up with a way to describe it to someone who cannot see the screen.

How can YOU use this exercise, or a variation, in your program?

Chat Exercise 4

LEADING QUESTIONS

Exercise Name	Leading Questions
Type of Exercise	Content Review
Required Tool Functionality	Group chat Ability to paste text into chat Ability to copy text out of chat and onto whiteboard (optional)
Instructional Objective/Purpose	To allow all participants to have their opinions heard before fully exploring the situation of one individual
Timing	Up to ten minutes

Design Considerations and Exercise Set-Up

- In your word processor, create a series of questions or statements for participants to respond to based on the content reviewed before or during class. For example, for a module on giving effective recognition, the statements might be
  1. Identify an opportunity for giving recognition.
  2. Describe the behavior of the person who deserves recognition as immediately and specifically as possible.
  3. State how the behavior made a difference to you and to the organization.
- Create a whiteboard with a header related to the content—in this case "Giving Recognition."
- Assign participants an independent assignment before class asking them to answer these same three questions in their participant guides.

Trainer Instructions

- Open the word processing document.
- Explain to participants that you will be posting a series of questions in the chat area. You will post a new question every thirty seconds or so.

They should answer the question based on their answers to the independent assignment.

- When participants have had the opportunity to answer all the questions, give them a minute to review their peers' responses. Give them an opportunity to comment on others' responses or question their peers.
- Select the response from one participant, copy the text, and paste it on the whiteboard.
- As a large group (using audio), discuss ways to help that participant meet his or her goal—in this case giving recognition to the identified colleague.

Producer Instructions

The producer can assist by:

- Pasting the questions into the chat area.

Participant Instructions

Directions to participants should be concise and easy to understand. Verbally instruct participants on what they will be doing. Consider including exercise instructions in the participant guide.

- Complete the independent work and be ready to respond to the questions.
- Review your peers' responses closely and give as much feedback as possible.

Exercise Notes and Variations

- The questions can be typed into the chat area and responses typed onto the whiteboard instead of copied and pasted. This takes a lot more time and doesn't eliminate typographical errors, but is necessary if your chat doesn't support copying and pasting text.

How can YOU use this exercise, or a variation, in your program?

 Chat Exercise 5

LET'S TALK!!!

Exercise Name	Let's Talk!!!
Type of Exercise	Communication skills
Required Tool Functionality	Group chat
Instructional Objective/Purpose	To allow all participants to respond to an audio-based scenario
Timing	Five minutes

Design Considerations and Exercise Set-Up

- Consider the example of a "Giving Effective Feedback" course.
- The instructional designer has to create a series of audio-based scenarios representing effective feedback and ineffective feedback. Two ways to accomplish this are
  - Record Internet audio files and play them back during your live program. (Make sure you test how this might work with your specific virtual classroom.)
  - Create a script that is read by the trainer with the assistance of participant volunteers or the assistant trainer. If using participant volunteers, the script needs to be printed in the participant guide.
- While the script is being read or audio being played, the screen should contain photographs of the characters represented in the role play.
- After each scenario, participants are directed to answer questions in the chat concerning what they just heard. For example:
  - How should Ronnie respond to Jack?
  - What could Jack have said differently to encourage a more positive response?

Trainer Instructions

- Instruct the participants to listen to the scenario.
- After the scenario is over, launch a slide containing questions about the scenario they just heard.

- Debrief the answers provided in the chat by providing appropriate responses.
- If appropriate, ask a participant to verbally express what he or she thinks is the "correct" response.
- Repeat for the next scenario.

Producer Instructions

The producer can assist by:

- Participating as a voice in the scenario.

Participant Instructions

Directions to participants should be concise and easy to understand. Verbally instruct participants on what they will be doing. Consider including exercise instructions in the participant guide.

- Take notes in your participant guides about what you hear in the scenario.
- Be ready to verbally express the correct response if asked.

Exercise Notes and Variations

- Consider breaking the class up into teams and sending them to breakout rooms to role play scenarios and receive feedback from their peers in the breakout rooms.

How can YOU use this exercise, or a variation, in your program?

6

Breakout Room Exercises and Techniques

Breakout rooms can most closely be compared to small-group interactions in a traditional classroom. In these types of exercises, the small groups work together at their own table and the trainer moves from group to group to assist them. Often, each group has its own flip chart and markers to capture the results of its discussion. Someone in the group may be asked to be the scribe, and someone else may be asked to report back to the larger group. All of these features are available in online breakout rooms.

This powerful online feature allows, at the discretion of the trainer, small groups to meet and share information during a larger synchronous session. Generally, the same tools are available in breakout rooms as are available in the full classroom. In some products, the only obvious indication that you have moved from the large class to the breakout room is the reduction in the number of people in your group.

Designing and facilitating effective breakout exercises requires advanced skills. Because breakout rooms are not used as often as other tools, designers may not be as familiar with how the tool works. Trainers have had another layer of separation placed between them and their participants. Not only is eye contact and body language not available, but now the participants are distributed among several virtual classrooms. Because of this, I strongly recommend that a producer be used to assist with the facilitation of any breakout exercise.

Once in a breakout room, you can assign participants a variety of exercises using other tools like the whiteboard or synchronized web browser. It is important to remember that breakout rooms are essentially just classrooms with fewer people. The limiting factors are your trainer's ability to facilitate these distributed groups and your participants' ability to manage the technology and work without a trainer in the same virtual space.

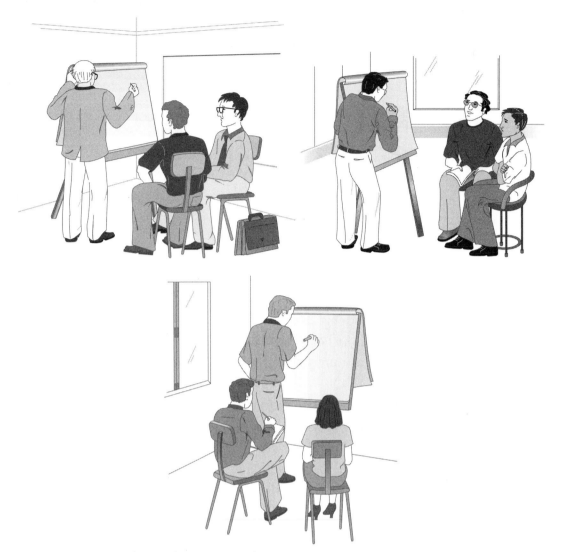

FIGURE 6.1 Traditional Group Work.

While using this tool, I have noticed two things:

1. In general, participants don't follow instructions very well. When participants are placed into a breakout room, they very often wait for the trainer to show up to reissue instructions or manage the tools for them.

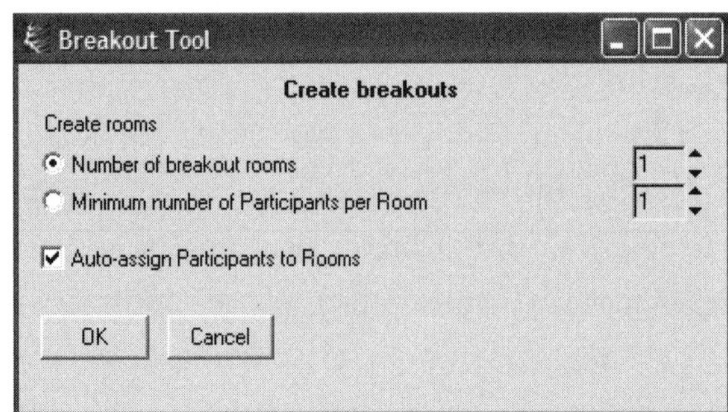

FIGURE 6.2 Illustration of Breakout Room.

2. In general, trainers don't deliver instructions very well. In a classroom situation, we know that we can easily see when a group is having difficulty and we know that we can walk over and assist them. Instructions need to be much more clear and concise when participants are geographically separated, not just from each other but from the trainer.

Instructional Uses

Here are some basic ideas to help the instructional designer create collaborative exercises using breakout rooms. More detailed examples are provided at the end of this chapter.

- Breakout rooms are ideal for training sessions in which teams or groups can share specific content. If you have an audience containing several groups (people from different companies or different professions, for example), you can assign each group to its own breakout room to explore case studies or problems that are customized for its needs.
- Team competitions can be conducted. Break up your participants into competitive teams and send them to the breakout rooms for a whiteboard, application sharing, or web browsing exercise. The team that gets the most right answers is the winner.
- Participants can be assigned to individual breakout rooms to complete a self-paced exercise or assessment. If your platform doesn't limit the number of breakout rooms, give participants the opportunity to work alone for a while. The trainer and producer can move through the individual rooms and provide assistance when necessary.
- You can work with groups or individuals on an as-needed basis.
- If there are varying levels of expertise in a class, a program can be divided and different trainers can moderate the breakout rooms.

Tool Variations and Considerations

Not all breakout rooms are the same. Each product has its own variation and conceptualization of how the tool works most effectively. Before designing exercises, it is important to thoroughly understand the intricacies of your specific tool. Here are some questions you should ask before designing collaborative breakout exercises.

- *What features (whiteboards, application sharing, and others) are available in the breakout rooms?* Often, breakout rooms are replicas of the synchronous classroom, and all collaboration tools are available.

- *How many breakout rooms can you have?* Some products allow as many breakout rooms as there are participants to allow for potential independent work. Others have a limit of three or four rooms.
- *How can participants and trainer communicate when they are not in the same room?* When participants run into problems, they need to be able to signal the trainer to come and help them. This is often accomplished using private chat. If the trainer wants to send a message to all breakout rooms, does he or she need to move to each room individually, or can some kind of broadcast message be sent to all rooms concurrently?
- *How are participants assigned to breakout rooms?* If you know the demographics of the individuals prior to the event, it can save time to assign individuals before the class starts. Because that information is not always available, it is more common for groups to be determined during the live event. If the group make-up is not important, you might be able to allow the software to assign people to individual rooms.
- *Can content be preassigned?* You may be able to assign different content for each group. For example, you might have a class comprised of salespeople, managers, and customer service representatives. If you assign them to breakout rooms by job title, it may be appropriate for each group to work on a case study appropriate for that job.
- *Can participants be moved from room to room during an activity?* Group dynamics change as new people join and existing members move out. If you can move people from room to room during the activity, you can create activities that take advantage of changing group dynamics. For example, give every group a different problem to solve. Every five minutes, rotate the group leaders from room to room and ask them to pick up solving a problem where the previous group leader left off.
- *Can materials (whiteboards and so on) created in breakout rooms be shared when the large group is reconvened?* Being able to access materials created in breakout rooms from the main classroom can be very useful in debriefing the exercise.
- *Can breakouts be recorded?* Most platforms are able to record the main classroom. Recording breakout rooms can be more complicated, and individual participants may need to manage this.

Best Practices and Techniques

Keep these tips in mind when designing and facilitating breakout interactions.

- Participants in breakout rooms often need assistance or reassurance. The trainer or producer should "drop in" regularly to provide guidance.
- If you are using an audioconferencing call (as opposed to Internet audio that is integrated into your classroom), you may need to rely on chat for communications between breakout participants. Another option is to set up separate conference calls for each breakout group.
- Have your producer set up and assign participants to the breakout rooms. This will save time during the class and help to ensure a smooth transition into and out of the smaller groups.
- You generally have the opportunity to assign a breakout room leader. During the live class, try to identify those participants who are most comfortable using the technology, and consider placing them in charge. The producer can help with this identification, leaving the trainer free to concentrate on content and facilitation.
- If you have a multi-session program that includes several breakout exercises, ask for volunteers before the event begins. Invite those volunteers for an additional technology training session so that they feel comfortable in the breakout session.
- Explain the breakout exercise to the large group, and then include technical and exercise instructions in printed materials so that participants understand what is expected of them and how they are supposed to accomplish it.
- Implement ground rules. When providing exercise instructions, make sure participants understand the following guidelines (and add whatever additional guidelines you feel are necessary!):
  - If you run into technical problems, contact the facilitator or producer. Don't waste a lot of time trying to solve them yourselves.
  - Assign someone to manage the exercise, someone to capture information, and someone to report back to the larger group.
  - Don't leave the breakout session just because the trainer isn't "watching" you.
  - When using collaboration tools within the breakout rooms (whiteboard, chat, application sharing, web browsing) the ground rules for those tools apply.

Sample Exercises

The rest of this chapter contains five detailed examples of breakout exercises. Sometimes, an assistant trainer, or producer, can be very helpful in facilitating these exercises. Because of this, instructions have been included for the trainer, producer, and participants.

Many chat, whiteboard, and application sharing exercises that work well for a large group are just as effective for breakout scenarios. Review the examples in other chapters for additional ideas.

Before designing comparable exercises for your initiatives, make sure you consider the software variations of your specific platform and test the exercises in a realistic setting. You may need to make accommodations for your particular synchronous platform.

In general, trainer and producer (assistant trainer) instructions will be available in a leader guide. Participant instructions will be delivered by the trainer verbally and will be supported by screen instructions and participant guide references when appropriate. A sample leader guide is located in Appendix E, and a sample participant guide is located in Appendix F.

At the end of each exercise there is room for you to take notes on how you may be able to customize the interaction for your specific projects. Make sure you keep track of the new ways you find to use the tools to collaborate online.

Breakout Room Exercise 1

INDEPENDENT STUDY

Exercise Name	Independent Study
Type of Exercise	Independent study or lab work
Required Tool Functionality	The ability for each participant to be assigned to a private breakout room
Instructional Objective/Purpose	To allow participants to work independently to practice a skill and to call in a trainer as needed
Timing	Ten to fifteen minutes

Design Considerations and Exercise Set-Up

- Ensure that participants have access to any required applications from their desktops.
- Create specific instructions and outcomes for the independent exercise. Include this information in the participant guide.
- The participant guide should also include instructions on how to launch any required tools (for example, application sharing) and how to contact the trainer for assistance.
- Create a whiteboard screen that will be available in the breakout room with reminders about what is to be accomplished.
- Consider the example (Figure 6.3) of a training program that teaches participants to use Word™ templates to create legal documents like a Power of Attorney or Last Will and Testament.
  1. While in the breakout room, each participant will launch Word and open the template for a Last Will and Testament.
  2. Using instructions and data located in the participant guide, participants will complete the template and save the resulting document to their hard drives.
  3. The trainer will assist each participant individually by visiting each room. If a participant needs immediate assistance, he or she should contact the trainer using chat or text messaging.
  4. If they complete the exercise before time is up, they can move on to the next template exercise in their guide.

Breakout Instructions
• Launch Word™ and open the template for a Last Will and Testament.
• Using instructions and data located in your Participant Guide, complete the template and save the resulting document to your computer.
• If you need help, contact me using private chat.
• If you complete the exercise before time is up, move on to the next template.
10 minutes

FIGURE 6.3 Sample Exercise.

Trainer Instructions

- Explain the objective of the breakout room exercise. Refer to the instructions in the participant guide so participants know where they can find additional assistance.
- Remind participants how to contact you while in a breakout room (private chat or other method).
- After the breakout rooms have been launched, continuously move from room to room to assist as necessary and to ensure that participants are on track.

Producer Instructions

The producer can assist by:

- Assigning participants to breakout rooms.
- Moving from room to room at the beginning of the exercise to make sure that no one is lost.
- Monitoring the private chat and being available to assist participants while the trainer is engaged with someone else.
- Broadcasting announcements to everyone, for example, giving a two-minute warning.

Participant Instructions

Directions to participants should be concise and easy to understand. Verbally instruct participants on what they will be doing. Consider including exercise instructions in the participant guide.

- Do not leave your computers while in the breakout rooms.
- Refer to the participant guide for instructions.
- Remember to ask for help!

How can YOU use this exercise, or a variation, in your program?

 **Breakout Room Exercise 2**

TRIADS

Exercise Name	Triads
Type of Exercise	Skills Practice
Required Tool Functionality	Multiple breakout rooms with three people each Ability for one person to talk while another writes on the whiteboard
Instructional Objective/Purpose	The ability to practice learned skills and receive feedback from your peers
Timing	Up to thirty minutes

Design Considerations and Exercise Set-Up

- This exercise is particularly effective when teaching business skills such as giving and receiving feedback or conducting a performance review.
- Participants should complete an independent exercise prior to the live event. This exercise prepares them to role play a personal scenario with a partner in the breakout room.
- Create specific instructions and outcomes for the triad exercise. Include this information in the participant guide.
- The participant guide should also include instructions on how to launch any required tools (for example, whiteboard tools), how to assign permissions to speak and write, and how to contact the trainer for assistance.
- In the participant guide, define the responsibilities of the triad.
  1. The "person practicing" should explain his or her personal scenario and role play his or her part based on the independent exercise completed prior to the live event.
  2. The "practice partner" will play the role assigned to him or her by the "person practicing" in the role play.
  3. The "coach" will observe the interactions, check off that all required components of the scenario are completed, and give feedback to the "person practicing" when he or she has finished.
- Create a whiteboard screen (Figure 6.4) that will be available in the breakout room with reminders about what is to be accomplished during the scenario.

In Your Breakout Rooms
The following instructions will help you participate in your breakout rooms. Each Learners' Role: • Perform your role in the practice session: Player #1, Practice Partner #2, or Observer. • Notify your facilitator before you step out. You need to be reassigned to the breakout room when you return. • Let your group members finish speaking before you start. ....

FIGURE 6.4 Sample Exercise.

Trainer Instructions

- Explain to participants that they will be assigned to breakout rooms in groups of three. One person will be the "person practicing," another the "practice partner," and another will be the "coach."
- Tell participants they have ten minutes to conduct the role play and give feedback, and then they should switch roles. The groups should go through the process three times.
- Refer to the instructions in the participant guide so participants know where they can find additional assistance.
- Remind participants how to contact you while in a breakout room (private chat, instant messaging, or other means).
- After the breakout rooms have been launched, continuously move from room to room to assist as necessary and to ensure that participants are on track.
- When the breakout rooms have ended, debrief the exercise.

Producer Instructions

The producer can assist by:

- Assigning participants to breakout rooms.
- Moving from room to room at the beginning of the exercise to make sure that no one is lost.

- Monitoring the private chat and being available to assist participants while the trainer is engaged with someone else.
- Broadcasting announcements to everyone, for example, giving a reminder every ten minutes for participants to switch roles.

Participant Instructions

Directions to participants should be concise and easy to understand. Verbally instruct participants on what they will be doing. Consider including exercise instructions in the participant guide.

- Do not leave your computers while in the breakout rooms.
- Refer to the participant guide for instructions.
- Participate fully, even when you are not the "person practicing."
- Remember to ask for help if you need it!

Exercise Notes and Variations

- If there is no reason to role play, take out the "practice partner" role. The "person practicing" can share information with the "coach" and receive feedback in a two-person breakout room.

How can YOU use this exercise, or a variation, in your program?

 Breakout Room Exercise 3

WORKING IN TEAMS

Exercise Name	Working in Teams
Type of Exercise	Team Discussion
Required Tool Functionality	Breakout rooms Two-way audio
Instructional Objective/Purpose	To allow teams with something in common to discuss specific content To encourage collaboration within a team
Timing	Varies

Design Considerations and Exercise Set-Up

- The trainer will need to have some demographic information about the participants in order to assign them to groups. For example, do they represent several distinct job functions? Are there individuals representing management as well as non-management employees? Are participants attending from several different companies? Is it a sales team representing different regions?
- Prior to the program, the trainer should preassign participants to breakout rooms representing the identified groups, if possible.
- A printed list of the group membership should be available to both the trainer and producer.
- Consider the example of an expense reduction training program (Figure 6.5). The exercise steps might look like this:
  1. Break the group into teams representing sales, office support, and production.
  2. Each breakout room has content specific to the monthly budget of each team.
  3. Each team is instructed to brainstorm ways to save $5,000 in expenses over a one-month period.

		Budget	Actual	Difference ($)	Difference (%)
PERSONNEL	Office			$0	0.0%
	Store			0	0.0%
	Salespeople			0	0.0%
	Others			0	0.0%
OPERATING	Advertising			$0	0.0%
	Bad debts			0	0.0%
	Cash discounts			0	0.0%
	Delivery costs			0	0.0%
	Depreciation			0	0.0%
	Dues and subscriptions			0	0.0%
	Employee benefits			0	0.0%
	Insurance			0	0.0%
	Interest			0	0.0%
	Legal and auditing			0	0.0%
	Maintenance and repairs			0	0.0%
	Office supplies			0	0.0%
	Postage			0	0.0%
	Rent or mortgage			0	0.0%
	Sales expenses			0	0.0%
	Shipping and storage			0	0.0%
	Supplies			0	0.0%
	Taxes			0	0.0%
	Telephone			0	0.0%
	Utilities			0	0.0%
	Other			0	0.0%
TOTAL EXPENSES		$0	$0	$0	0.0%

FIGURE 6.5 Sample Exercise.

Trainer Instructions

- Explain the objective of the breakout room exercise, for example, "While in the breakout room, each group will identify ways to save $5,000 a month in expenses."
- Refer to the instructions in the participant guide so participants know where they can find additional assistance.
- Remind participants how to contact you while in a breakout room (private chat or other means).
- After the breakout rooms have been launched, continuously move from room to room to assist as necessary and to ensure that participants are on track.

Producer Instructions

The producer can assist by:

- Assigning participants to breakout rooms.

- Moving from room to room at the beginning of the exercise to make sure that no one is lost.
- Monitoring the private chat and being available to assist participants while the trainer is engaged with someone else.
- Broadcasting announcements to everyone, for example, giving a two-minute warning for the participants to finish the activity.

Participant Instructions

Directions to participants should be concise and easy to understand. Verbally instruct participants on what they will be doing. Consider including exercise instructions in the participant guide.

- Do not leave your computers while in the breakout rooms.
- Someone should volunteer to lead the discussion and someone should volunteer to capture information on the whiteboard.
- Refer to the participant guide for instructions.
- Participate fully, and support the team initiative.
- Remember to ask for help if you need it!

Exercise Notes and Variations

- If there are only two groups, the trainer can stay with one group to observe and assist, and the producer can stay with the other.
- If participants aren't skilled with the tools, suggest that the person capturing information use the chat area or paper and pen instead of the whiteboard.
- Consider allowing the groups to continue collaboration when the debriefing is complete. For example, if the group identified five problems, send them back to the rooms to brainstorm possible solutions.

How can YOU use this exercise, or a variation, in your program?

Breakout Exercise 4

GROUP SCAVENGER HUNT

Exercise Name	Group Scavenger Hunt
Type of Exercise	Discovery Exercise/Instructional Game
Required Tool Functionality	Breakout rooms
Instructional Objective/Purpose	To provide an opportunity for a group to work together to debrief content as a team
Timing	Ten minutes

Design Consideration and Exercise Set-Up

- Participants should complete an independent exercise that informs about content related to the course objectives.
- Consider the example of a sexual harassment awareness training program. The exercise steps might look like this:
  1. Create a series of ten questions dealing with the subject of sexual harassment in the workplace. Answers to these questions should be available via a variety of means, including on the Internet, in the participant materials, or even from the trainer.
  2. These questions should NOT be in the participant guide. They should only be available on a whiteboard screen that will be shown in the breakout room so participants do not try to find the answers ahead of time. (See Figure 6.6.)

Trainer Instructions

- Explain the objective of the breakout room exercise, for example, while in the breakout room, the group participants will collaborate to answer

Scavenger Hunt Answer the Following Questions
1. When is an employer legally responsible for harassment by a supervisor?
2. What should employers do to **prevent and correct harassment**?
3. Does an employee who is harassed by his or her supervisor have any **responsibilities**?

FIGURE 6.6 Sample Exercise.

the questions. They may use participant materials, the Internet, or each other—any resource they can think of. (Resourceful groups may think of asking other groups or even the trainer!)

- Refer to the instructions in the participant guide so participants know where they can find additional assistance.
- Verbally remind participants how to contact you while in a breakout room (private chat or other means).
- After the breakout rooms have been launched, continuously move from room to room to assist as necessary and to ensure that participants are on track.

Producer Instructions

The producer can assist by:

- Assigning participants to breakout rooms.
- Moving from room to room at the beginning of the exercise to make sure that no one is lost.
- Explaining to participants how to use resources and tools that will help them to answer the questions.
- Monitoring the private chat and being available to assist participants while the trainer is engaged with someone else.
- Broadcasting announcements to everyone, for example, giving a two-minute warning for the participants to finish the activity.

Participant Instructions

Directions to participants should be concise and easy to understand. Verbally instruct participants on what they will be doing. Consider including exercise instructions in the participant guide.

- You should not leave your computers while in the breakout rooms.
- Someone should volunteer to lead the discussion and someone should volunteer to capture information on the whiteboard.
- Refer to the participant guide for instructions.
- Participate fully, and support the team initiative.
- Remember to ask for help if you need it!

Exercise Notes and Variations

- This can easily be made into a contest. The team with the most correct answers in the least amount of time wins the contest.
- The entire scavenger hunt can be conducted via synchronized web browsing.
- This does not need to be content-related. It can be made into an icebreaker or team-building activity using questions unrelated to the content.

How can YOU use this exercise, or a variation, in your program?

Breakout Room Exercise 5

TEACHING ON TWO LEVELS

Exercise Name	Teaching on Two Levels
Type of Exercise	Remediation
Required Tool Functionality	Breakout room
Instructional Objective/Purpose	This is a way to allow a more skilled group to discuss the application of content while the rest of the class "catches up"
Timing	Varies

Design Considerations and Set-Up

- This design can be applied if a pretest shows that there are two distinct groups of learners.
- Consider the example of a class that teaches participants how to send email messages, use an instant messenger program, and post to a discussion board. There are ten participants enrolled in the class. Based on a pre-assessment, it is discovered that:
  - Four participants have mastered the use of email, but have little or no experience with using instant messenger and discussion boards.
  - Six participants have little or no experience with any of the tools.
- A series of discussion questions about the appropriate use of email should be prepared for the group that has mastered email.

Trainer Instructions

- Explain that the group will be split up during the email discussion, but reassembled to discuss the other topics.
- Send the advanced group to a breakout room with instructions to answer the discussion questions presented in that room.
- At the same time, the trainer should work with the remaining participants to cover the information about using email. This information can be reinforced in participant materials.
- The entire group should then be reconvened to discuss the next agenda items: instant messenger and discussion boards.

Producer Instructions

The producer can assist by:

- Assigning participants to breakout rooms.
- Moderating the advanced group discussion and managing the technology in the breakout room.
- Broadcasting announcements to everyone, for example, giving a two-minute warning for the participants to finish the activity.

Participant Instructions

Directions to participants should be concise and easy to understand. Verbally instruct participants on what they will be doing. Consider including exercise instructions in the participant guide.

- For those in the breakout discussion, be as participative as possible.

Exercise Notes and Variations

- If a subject-matter expert is in the class, he or she can work with the advanced group in a breakout room to answer questions about the real-life application of content. If you use this variation, little design time is needed.

How can YOU use this exercise, or a variation, in your program?

7

Application Sharing Exercises and Techniques

When purchasing a synchronous product, organizations often have the most questions about application sharing. This feature allows the trainer to share software applications (such as spreadsheets, word processing, or custom applications) with participants, even if the participants do not have the software installed on their individual machines. Because the feature is so visually impressive, vendors often use it as a highlight for their demonstrations.

There are many varieties of application sharing, ranging from "view only" on the participants' side to allowing participants to actually interact with applications shared by the trainer or by other participants.

Although the feature is very powerful, it is often not used creatively. The most common application is demonstrating software and allowing one or two participants to replicate what they saw the trainer do. This is useful in some circumstances—but it does not promote participant collaboration or provide the opportunity for all participants to learn how to use the software. There are many ways to use application sharing that do successfully teach in a collaborative manner.

Because working with an application during a sharing exercise often takes the trainer's focus away from the virtual classroom, it is very helpful to have a producer to monitor feedback, questions, and interactions.

Instructional Uses

Here are some basic ideas to help the instructional designer create collaborative exercises using application sharing. More detailed examples are provided at the end of this chapter.

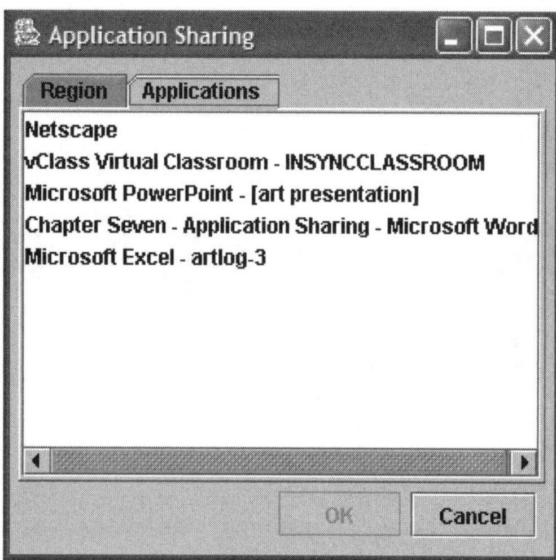

FIGURE 7.1 Selecting an Application in vClass.

- Use application sharing to demonstrate software features. This is the most common use of this tool and is a good starting point for other, more collaborative, application sharing exercises.
- Create a case study and pass control from participant to participant to complete steps in series. If information from previous steps is needed for later steps, it will encourage all participants to pay attention. Having everyone complete different tasks reduces tedium while teaching a process.
- Small groups can collaborate by sharing common office software packages in the breakout rooms. For example, you may want a sales group to determine the best sales mix for their territory during the next twelve months. Give them access to a spreadsheet file and have them collaborate using the spreadsheet.
- Participants can use application sharing in individual breakout rooms. This allows them to interact with an application residing on their own desktops. If the bandwidth is available, each individual can work in his or her own breakout room on an application and receive personal assistance from a trainer.
- Application sharing can be a very powerful role-playing tool for teaching skills that involve technology. A single participant can interact with the technology based on a case study or mock telephone call while the other participants watch and provide feedback.

Tool Variations and Considerations

Not all application sharing tools are the same. Each product has its own variation and conceptualization of how the tool works most effectively.

Before designing exercises, it is important to thoroughly understand the intricacies of your specific tool. Here are some questions you should ask before designing collaborative application sharing exercises.

- *What types of applications can be shared?* If you have an older or very large application, it may not share well or at all. Ask your vendor about limitations, and be sure to test for effectiveness before creating exercises.
- *Can the entire desktop be shared?* Some synchronous platforms only allow you to share an entire desktop. Some offer desktop sharing as an option. You want to be sure of how to use these capabilities so you can design your exercises with a mind to what the participants will be seeing. You need to plan whether they can see the entire desktop, the entire application, or just a fixed window size of an application.
- *What are the bandwidth requirements for application sharing?* The more items you are sharing, the bigger the impact on bandwidth. If you have five breakout rooms in process, each sharing its own application, it could be more than your network can gracefully manage.
- *Can participants interact with the application or just view it?* While most vendors offer a full application sharing option, some only allow the participants to observe the trainer interacting with the application.
- *Can applications be shared from a participant's desktop?* There are some circumstances, such as in software development courses, in which the class can benefit from viewing an application shared from a participant's machine.

Best Practices and Techniques

Keep these tips in mind when designing and facilitating breakout interactions.

The author would like to thank Margaret Driscoll at IBM Lotus Software and Curtis Rockey of Rockey & Associates for generously contributing so many of these best practices. Many tips have been adapted (or taken verbatim!) with permission from the article "20 Best Practices for Using Application Sharing" (Driscoll & Rockey, 2002).

- Plan for "technology gaps." When launching an application there is often a gap of up to thirty seconds. This "dead air" is enough to make your less secure participants wonder if they are experiencing technical difficulties and prompt your less tolerant participants to jump into an unrelated task. Anticipate that gap, and design a meaningful personal or chat activity to fill the time.

- Evaluate when to use and not use application sharing. Application sharing may not be the best way to teach a complicated application with lots of steps or applications that require practice. For example, learning to use Flash™ may be better taught as a self-paced course where students can work at their own pace and engage in drill and practice.
- Use the long method. Avoid using shortcuts and smart keys because learners find it easier to follow you through a series of pulldown menus. For example if you were teaching how to use *cut*, don't use [CTRL]+[X]; instead, tell learners to go to Edit, expand menu, and select Cut.
- Tell learners where to look. Think of this as a narrative tour. As you move your mouse around the screen, tell learners where to look. For example, tell the learner to look at the top left for the edit menu and explain when you are clicking, dragging, and pulling down.
- Optimize the visibility of the mouse. Go to Start menu → Settings → Control panels → Mouse to change the properties of size, shape, and color to make it as visible as possible.
- Plan for latency. Latency describes the effect of screens repainting at different speeds for students at different locations on the Internet. Be prepared to stop and check that everyone is looking at the same application screen.
- Determine student viewing area. Prior to the session, look at a student's view of the application sharing tool and determine how much space there is. Then, when you are sharing the application, make your window the same size. This way, you will only refer to screen elements the students can see without scrolling.
- Use the page up and page down keys. To move up and down in the application you are sharing, use the paging keys. By using these keys instead of scrolling, the participant's screen will render new images more quickly and clearly.
- Implement ground rules. When providing exercise instructions, make sure participants understand the following guidelines (and add whatever additional guidelines you feel are necessary!):
    - Apply window management. If you are sharing your entire desktop, close any windows that you do not need. Closing all the unnecessary windows will help focus attention.
    - Ask permission. When assuming control of another's shared application, be sure to ask permission. Seeing someone drive an application on his or her secure PC environment may be a new experience for many participants, and it is good to ensure it is a comfortable one.

Sample Exercises

The rest of this chapter contains five detailed examples of application sharing exercises. Sometimes an assistant trainer, or producer, can be very helpful in facilitating these exercises. Because of this, instructions have been included for the trainer, producer, and participants.

Before designing comparable exercises for your initiatives, make sure you consider the software variations of your specific platform and test the exercises in a realistic setting. You may have to make accommodations for your particular synchronous platform.

In general, trainer and producer (assistant trainer) instructions will be available in a leader guide. Participant instructions will be delivered by the trainer verbally and will be supported by screen instructions and participant guide references when appropriate. A sample leader guide is located in Appendix E, and a sample participant guide is located in Appendix F.

At the end of each exercise, there is room for you to take notes on how you may be able to customize the interaction for your specific projects. Make sure you keep track of the new ways you find to use the tools to collaborate online.

 Application Sharing Exercise 1

INDEPENDENT STUDY

Exercise Name	Independent Study
Type of Exercise	Independent study or lab work
Required Tool Functionality	The ability for each participant to be assigned to a private breakout room
Instructional Objective/Purpose	To allow participants to work independently to practice a skill and to call in a trainer as needed
Timing	Ten to fifteen minutes

Note: This exercise is also introduced in Chapter 6 as Breakout Room Exercise 1.

Design Considerations and Exercise Set-Up

- Ensure that participants have access to any required applications from their desktops. Since participants will be working independently in the breakout rooms, they need access to their own applications.
- Create specific instructions and outcomes for the independent exercise. Include this information in the participant guide.
- The participant guide should also include instructions on how to launch any required tools, especially application sharing, and how to contact the trainer for assistance.
- Create a whiteboard screen that will be available in the breakout room with reminders about what is to be accomplished.
- Consider the example of a training program that teaches participants to use Word templates to create legal documents like a Power of Attorney or Last Will and Testament. You want individual participants to learn how to use these Word templates, but want to be able to individually review accomplishments and provide one-on-one assistance as necessary.
  1. While in the breakout room, each participant will launch Word and open the template for a Last Will and Testament. When an individual

launches Word from within a breakout room, he or she is utilizing the application sharing feature of the virtual classroom.

2. Using instructions and data located in the participant guide, participants will complete the template and save the resulting document to their hard drives.
3. The trainer will assist each participant individually by visiting each room. If a participant needs immediate assistance, he or she should contact the trainer using chat or text messaging.
4. If they complete the exercise before time is up, they can move on to the next template exercise in their guide.

Trainer Instructions

- Explain the objective of the application sharing exercise. Refer to the instructions in the participant guide so participants know where they can find additional assistance.
- Remind participants how to contact the trainer while in a breakout room (private chat or other means).
- After the breakout rooms have been launched, continuously move from room to room to assist as necessary and to ensure that participants are on track.

Producer Instructions

The producer can assist by:

- Assigning participants to breakout rooms.
- Moving from room to room at the beginning of the exercise to make sure that no one is lost.
- Monitoring the private chat and being available to assist participants while the trainer is engaged with someone else.
- Broadcasting announcements to everyone, for example, giving a two-minute warning.

Participant Instructions

Directions to participants should be concise and easy to understand. Verbally instruct participants on what they will be doing. Consider including exercise instructions in the participant guide.

- Do not leave your computers while in the breakout rooms.
- Refer to the participant guide for instructions.
- Remember to ask for help if you need it!

How can YOU use this exercise, or a variation, in your program?

Application Sharing Exercise 2

TELEPHONE REP ROLE PLAY

Exercise Name	Telephone Rep Role Play
Type of Exercise	Skills Practice
Required Tool Functionality	Application sharing
Instructional Objective/Purpose	To allow a participant to role play a customer service situation that requires both telephone interaction skills and data entry skills
Timing	Five to ten minutes

Design Considerations and Exercise Set-Up

- Consider the example (Figure 7.2) of teaching a customer service representative to enter data into a software system while on the telephone. It is especially effective because participants can watch the data entry process while listening to the interaction between the role players.
- The trainer must be prepared to play the part of a customer calling in to update information in a system, lodge a complaint, or whatever. These scenarios have to be written out in the leader guide.

Trainer Instructions

- Launch the desired application and turn over control to the participant who will be the first role play participant.

FIGURE 7.2 Sample Exercise.

- Start the role play by saying "Hello. I am calling about. . . ."
- Stay "on the phone," following the lead of the role-play participant, until the participant feels he or she has completed the transaction.
- Debrief the exercise by first asking the role-play participant about what worked well and what was difficult, then by asking for the rest of the participants to provide feedback, and finally by providing your own feedback on the interaction.

Producer Instructions

The producer can assist by:

- Monitoring chat questions while the trainer is involved in the role play.

Participant Instructions

Directions to participants should be concise and easy to understand. Verbally instruct participants on what they will be doing. Consider including exercise instructions in the participant guide.

- If you are role playing, respond to the trainer as if you were in a live transaction. Input data into the shared system as appropriate.
- If you are observing, make observations and take notes about the interaction and be ready to provide feedback about the role play.

Exercise Notes and Variations

- Make sure you have a different scenario for each participant.
- Consider asking participants to play the part of the caller. This makes the program more participative and less rehearsed. (You will need to provide participants with scenario instructions.)
- Instead of running all of the role plays at once, intersperse them with other content and exercises to make the program seem less redundant.

How can YOU use this exercise, or a variation, in your program?

Application Sharing Exercise 3

DEMONSTRATION AND DESKTOP PRACTICE

Exercise Name	Demonstration and Desktop Practice
Type of Exercise	Independent Study
Required Tool Functionality	Application sharing
Instructional Objective/Purpose	To allow participants to practice working with an application that they just saw demonstrated
Timing	Five minutes

Design Considerations and Exercise Set-Up

- This is a way for all participants to practice with an application at the same time while minimizing the impact on bandwidth.
- Since everyone will be working on individual exercises outside of the virtual classroom environment, ensure that participants have access to the required application from their desktops.
- Create specific instructions and outcomes for the application sharing exercise. Include this information in the participant guide.
- Create a whiteboard screen with reminders about what is to be accomplished.
- Consider the example (Figure 7.3) of an accounting software package training program. The exercise steps might look like this:
    1. Participants are instructed to open the software package on their own machines.
    2. Participants should input the data listed in their participant guides.
    3. Participants should create an income statement, balance sheet, and cash flow statement for the month ending June 30, 2004.
    4. In their participant guides, participants should write down the amount for owner's equity, liabilities, and office expenses based on the resulting reports.

Excel template   Template 1 of 1 Next

[Company Name] Balance Sheet		[DATE]	
Current ratio	3.38	Cash ratio	0.24
Quick ratio	2.91	Working capital	$3,761
ASSETS		LIABILITIES	
Current assets		**Current liabilities**	
Cash and cash equivalents	373	Loans payable and current portion long-term debt	38
Short-term investments	1,517	Accounts payable and accrued expenses	1,205
Accounts receivable	1,918	Income taxes payable	327
Inventories	743	Accrued retirement and profit-sharing contributions	10
Deferred income taxes	445		
Prepaid expenses and other current assets	345		
Total current assets	$5,341	Total current liabilities	$1,580
Other assets		**Other liabilities**	
Property, plant and equipment at cost	10,963	Long-term debt	2,345
Less accumulated depreciation	(3,098)	Accrued retirement costs	1,211
Property, plant and equipment (net)	6,495	Deferred income taxes	485
Long-term cash investments	472	Deferred credits and other liabilities	331
Equity investments	1,972		
Deferred income taxes	437		
Other assets	634		
Total other assets	$17,875	Total other liabilities	$4,372
Total assets	$23,216	Total liabilities	$5,952

FIGURE 7.3 Sample Exercise.

Trainer Instructions

- Demonstrate the application transaction and ask the participants for any questions.
- Remind participants that instructions are in the participant guide.
- Instruct participants to contact you using chat (not voice) during this exercise.
- Instruct participants to minimize (not close) the virtual class and launch the required application. Then complete the practice exercises in the participant guide.

Producer Instructions

The producer can assist by:

- Monitoring chat questions while the trainer is assisting individual participants.
- Assisting participants when necessary.

Participant Instructions

Directions to participants should be concise and easy to understand. Verbally instruct participants on what they will be doing. Consider including exercise instructions in the participant guide.

- Minimize (not close) the virtual class and launch the required application. Then complete the practice exercises in the participant guide.
- Do not leave your computers during this exercise.
- Refer to the participant guide for instructions.
- Remember to ask for help if you need it, using chat.

Exercise Notes and Variations

- If multiple participants are having similar problems, use audio to provide guidance to the entire group.

How can YOU use this exercise, or a variation, in your program?

 Application Sharing Exercise 4

APPLICATION ROUND ROBIN

Exercise Name	Application Round Robin
Type of Exercise	Case Study
Required Tool Functionality	Application sharing
Instructional Objective/Purpose	To involve all participants in a case study that demonstrates the use of an application
Timing	Ten minutes

Design Considerations and Exercise Set-Up

- Prepare a case study that involves a series of related transactional steps. Consider the example of a travel agent planning a trip using a reservation system. The steps might be as follows:
    1. Reserve a round trip ticket from Huntsville, Alabama, to Boston, Massachusetts, leaving January 1 and returning January 10.
    2. Reserve a non-smoking room at a $100 per night (approximate) hotel for this traveler.
    3. Reserve an economy car for this traveler.
    4. Change the return date on the airline ticket to January 14.
    5. Update the hotel reservation.
    6. Update the car rental reservation.
    7. Add a second traveler for the entire trip.

Trainer Instructions

- After demonstrating the application, give a participant permission to interact with the application and ask him or her to complete the first step of the transaction.
- When that participant is finished, give another participant permission to interact with the application and ask him or her to complete the second step.

- Repeat until all steps are demonstrated by participants.
- Ask for questions about the process.

Producer Instructions

The producer can assist by:

- Monitoring chat questions while the trainer is assisting individual participants.

Participant Instructions

Directions to participants should be concise and easy to understand. Verbally instruct participants on what they will be doing. Consider including exercise instructions in the participant guide.

- Pay attention to each step of the process. Since each transaction builds on the previous transaction, it is important that you understand what your peers accomplished before you.

Exercise Notes and Variations

- Add extra steps to include more participants.
- This can be effective in breakout rooms with smaller groups. Instructions would need to be included in the participant guide, and the trainer would move from room to room in order to facilitate the interaction.

How can YOU use this exercise, or a variation, in your program?

Application Sharing Exercise 5

MULTIMEDIA TRIVIA GAME

Exercise Name Multimedia Trivia Game

Type of Exercise Trivia Game

Required Tool Functionality Application sharing

Instructional Objective/Purpose To test participants on their knowledge of the content

Timing Five to ten minutes

Design Considerations and Exercise Set-Up

- This is an effective wrap-up to verify that lecture material was retained and understood.
- Consider the example (Figure 7.4) of product training. Have your multimedia department design a "game show" (modeling on shows like Jeopardy™ or Wheel of Fortune™) that incorporates facts about the products taught in a class.
- The game can be created in any multimedia program (Flash™, Authorware™, and so forth) that is supported by the organization's information technology group.
- A time limit should be determined and strictly enforced.

Trivia Game			
Customer Service	Leadership	Selling Techniques	Choice!!!
What are the 3 steps to answering the phone?	10 Points	10 Points	10 Points
20 Points	20 Points	20 Points	*Name 2 management courses mandated by law*
30 Points	30 Points	30 Points	30 Points

FIGURE 7.4 Sample Exercise.

Trainer Instructions

- Have the application launched and ready to share before the class begins.
- Launch the multimedia application through the application sharing tool.
- Announce the rules of the game and any potential prizes.
- Act as the "host" and conduct the game, alternating between participants.
- The individual or team with the most points at the end of the appointed time wins.

Producer Instructions

The producer can assist by:

- Monitoring chat questions while the trainer is facilitating the exercise.
- Keeping score.

Participant Instructions

Directions to participants should be concise and easy to understand. Verbally instruct participants on what they will be doing. Consider including exercise instructions in the participant guide.

- Use all resources available to you (participant guide, Internet sites, notes) to answer questions as quickly as possible.

Exercise Notes and Variations

- Off-the-shelf trivia computer games are available commercially and can be very effective for online exercises. Because the questions will be generic in nature, use it as a warm-up or icebreaker activity.
- If there are a lot of participants, pair people up and have them collaborate. They can brainstorm answers using private chat, if available.
- A nice "prize" for the winners is gift certificates in $5 increments from online vendors like Amazon.com.

How can YOU use this exercise, or a variation, in your program?

8

Synchonized Web Browsing Exercises and Techniques

When you think about it, you might consider synchronous platforms to be customized synchronized web browsers. Participants are logged on to a website, and they see web content (often in the form of uploaded PowerPoint slides) that the trainer wants them to see.

Within the virtual classroom, the feature of synchronized web browsing allows the trainer or participants to bring the class to an Internet site or corporate intranet. It provides the opportunity to use the entire World Wide Web as potential content in the classroom. This allows facilitators to browse the web while the participants follow them. As links are clicked or addresses entered into the URL locator, the websites will be launched on the participants' machines.

This is another highly demonstrated feature in the synchronous classroom sales process, but one that is frequently underutilized once such classes are implemented in organizations. (See Figure 8.1.)

Instructional Uses

Here are some basic ideas to help the instructional designer create collaborative exercises using synchronized web browsing. More detailed examples are provided at the end of this chapter.

- Instead of re-creating content that already exists, you can use the Internet or corporate intranet as a content source. This will be more visually interesting than slides and provide the participants with a place to go later to find more detailed information.
- One way to allow a participant to share information is to allow that participant to bring the class to a website.

FIGURE 8.1 Web Browsing Tool.

- Independent exercises located on a website can be initiated for the entire group—including web-enabled, self-paced exercises created in multimedia applications.
- Some synchronous applications require you to download content to a participant's machine ahead of time. In these cases, last-minute content can made available for an existing program by placing it on the web.
- The web can be used as the basis for scavenger hunt type games that can be used for icebreakers or contests.
- Use the web to teach about competitors, current events, or industry news. By using this method instead of preparing slides, you can ensure you always have the most up-to-date information.

Tool Variations and Considerations

Not all synchronized web browsers are the same. Each product has its own variation and conceptualization of how the tool works most effectively. Before designing exercises, it is important to thoroughly understand the intricacies of your specific tool. Here are some questions you should ask before designing collaborative web browsing exercises.

- *Is this a true "follow me" application?* In this situation, participants can see the sites the trainer initiates, but cannot access the embedded hyperlinks.
- *Can hyperlinks be made available to individual participants?* If this is the case, once on a site launched by a trainer, the participants can click through the links independently. To bring the class back together, the trainer usually needs to launch the next content item in the agenda.

Some synchronous packages support both the "follow me" feature and the ability for participants to navigate independently. For example, if you include an URL in the course agenda when assembling content (each software platform does this a little differently), participants may have independent navigation, but if you use application sharing to access your web browser, you are in a true "follow me" mode.

- *How are multimedia sites managed?* If you want to bring the class to a site that utilizes multimedia, such as Flash or Authorware, each participant may need to have the appropriate plug-in.
- *Can a participant bring the class to a website?* By allowing participants the chance to lead exercises, you have the opportunity to engage them and satisfy their need as adult learners to share personal experiences.
- *Can bookmarks be created prior to class?* If you can create bookmarks, it eliminates the time it takes to type in complicated URLs and minimizes the chances for typing errors.
- *Does this feature require a specific browser?* You may need to inform participants to log in using a specific web browser and to reset their default browser, depending on the requirements of the synchronous application. (Ask your vendor support desk for instructions.)

Best Practices and Techniques

Keep these tips in mind when designing and facilitating synchronous web browsing interactions.

- Check that URLs are current. Web addresses and content are dynamic and change often. Check the web addresses before each class to make sure all the necessary links are available.
- Check site policies. Many sites have "usage" policies. Read them to make sure you don't need permission to access the site.
- Ask for permission. Consider letting the webmaster know you are using the site for a course and asking for permission to link there.
- Make sure you can get to the site. You may not be able to visit sites that require a password. You also may not be able to visit secure sites (that is, any site for which the protocol begins with "https"). Some sites may be blocked by your organization's firewall.
- Ask participants to verify access through their firewalls. If you have participants from outside your network, consider sending the URLs to them ahead of time so that they can verify that their networks don't block the site.
- Bookmark. When a site is used, suggest that participants bookmark the URL or write down the address so they can access it again after the program.
- Provide clear instructions. If you have an exercise during which participants will navigate independently, include instructions and expected

outcomes in the participant guide. Don't leave your participants adrift in the World Wide Web!

- Implement ground rules. When providing exercise instructions, make sure participants understand the following guidelines (and add whatever additional guidelines you feel are necessary!):
  - When independent navigation of hyperlinks is available, don't start clicking until the trainer tells you to.
  - When leading the class to a website, be sensitive about the nature of the content.

Sample Exercises

The rest of this chapter contains four detailed examples of synchronized web browsing exercises. Sometimes an assistant trainer, or producer, can be very helpful in facilitating these exercises. Because of this, instructions have been included for the trainer, producer, and participants.

Before designing comparable exercises for your initiatives, make sure you consider the software variations of your specific platform and test the exercises in a realistic setting. You may need to make accommodations for your particular synchronous platform.

In general, trainer and producer (assistant trainer) instructions will be available in a leader guide. Participant instructions will be delivered by the trainer verbally and will be supported by screen instructions and participant guide references when appropriate. A sample leader guide is located in Appendix E, and a sample participant guide is located in Appendix F.

At the end of each exercise, there is room for you to take notes on how you may be able to customize the interaction for your specific projects. Make sure you keep track of the new ways you find to use the tools to collaborate online.

Synchronized Web Browsing Exercise 1

ONLINE TOOLS EXPLORATION

Exercise Name	Online Tools Exploration
Type of Exercise	Discovery
Required Tool Functionality	Synchronized web browser If participants click on a link on a web page, they are able to access that link independently of the rest of the class
Instructional Objective/Purpose	To allow a participant to explore a web-based tool located on your corporate intranet
Timing	Five minutes

Design Considerations and Exercise Set-Up

- This is a great way to teach participants about a web-based tool such as a help facility, training portal, or knowledge database.
- Prepare a set of questions for the participant guide that you would like answered during the exploration. These questions should ensure that participants visit every area of the site you want to expose them to.
- Consider the example of a competitive intelligence module in a sales training program. The exercise steps might look like this:
  1. The trainer will access the company's intranet and launch the competitive intelligence database.
  2. The participants will independently browse the database and answer the ten questions listed in their participant guides.

Trainer Instructions

- Bring participants to a website and explain its purpose. For example, a website might provide detailed online help about a custom application.
- Explain how to navigate through the website.
- Tell participants that they have five minutes to explore this site. While they are exploring, they must answer all of the questions listed in the participant guide.

- Ask participants to click the "YES" or "OK" button when they have completed their review.
- At the end of the exercise, launch a slide with the questions and ask for participants to volunteer the answers.
- Ask for questions about the online application.

Producer Instructions

The producer can assist by:

- Monitoring chat questions while the trainer is assisting individual participants.
- Providing a one-minute warning to inform participants about the amount of time they have left to finish the exercise.

Participant Instructions

Directions to participants should be concise and easy to understand. Verbally instruct participants about what they will be doing. Consider including exercise instructions in the participant guide.

- Do not leave your computers during this exercise.
- Explore the website and answer the questions listed in the participant guide.

Exercise Notes and Variations

- This can be an asynchronous exercise that participants complete before class.

How can YOU use this exercise, or a variation, in your program?

 **Synchronized Web Browser Exercise 2**

SEVEN DEGREES OF SEPARATION

Exercise Name	Seven Degrees of Separation
Type of Exercise	Group Discovery or Icebreaker
Required Tool Functionality	Synchronized web browser Participants should not be able to browse independently. They should follow the instructor as he or she navigates through the website.
Instructional Objective/Purpose	To demonstrate relationships between organizations, concepts, or problems.
Timing	Under five minutes

Design Considerations and Exercise Set-Up

- Sometimes it is important to illustrate how closely (or not!) two things are connected. For example, an organization may want to be closely tied with its suppliers.
- Create scenarios that help to illustrate this concept on the web. Sample scenarios might be
    - How many clicks does it take to connect our website with that of our closest competitors?
    - How many clicks does it take to connect the president of the United States with our state congressman?
- Make sure you have possible answers to all of your questions.

Trainer Instructions

- After launching the synchronized web browser, explain your scenario.
- Ask for one participant to provide a starting website.
- Ask another participant to suggest a link on that website that will take you one step closer to the desired connection.
- Repeat until you make the connection OR decide you've run into a dead end.

Producer Instructions

The producer can assist by:

- Keeping track of the links as they are suggested by participants.

Participant Instructions

Directions to participants should be concise and easy to understand. Verbally instruct participants on what they will be doing. Consider including exercise instructions in the participant guide.

- Think creatively and assist your peers if they get stuck!

Exercise Notes and Variations

- To remind participants of the connections you are trying to make, include them in the participant guide or post them in the chat area.

How can YOU use this exercise, or a variation, in your program?

 **Synchronized Web Browser Exercise 3**

ONLINE TESTING

Exercise Name	Online Testing
Type of Exercise	Test or Evaluation
Required Tool Functionality	Synchronized web browser Once at the website, participants should be able to browse independently
Instructional Objective/Purpose	To test knowledge or gather evaluation data
Timing	Five minutes

Design Considerations and Exercise Set-Up

- The online test or evaluation has to be created and posted to the Internet or intranet prior to the live event.
- Testing must be performed to ensure that:
  - Participants located outside the firewall can access tests located inside the firewall.
  - Participants located inside the firewall can access tests located outside the firewall.
- Participants may need to log on to the test or evaluation individually with a user name and password.
  - This procedure should be tested and documented in the participant guide.
  - User names and passwords should be distributed prior to the live event.

Trainer Instructions

- Bring the participants to the desired website and provide any special instructions for taking the test or completing the evaluation.

Producer Instructions

The producer can assist by:

- Broadcasting announcements to everyone, for example, giving a two-minute warning for the participants to finish the activity.

Participant Instructions

Directions to participants should be concise and easy to understand. Verbally instruct participants on what they will be doing. Consider including exercise instructions in the participant guide.

- Follow instructions provided by the trainer.

Exercise Notes and Variations

- You may also send the participants a link to the test or evaluation in an email after the program is over.

How can YOU use this exercise, or a variation, in your program?

 **Synchronized Web Browser Exercise 4**

ONLINE ORIENTATION

Exercise Name	Online Orientation
Type of Exercise	Web Content Overview
Required Tool Functionality	Synchronized web browser
Instructional Objective/Purpose	To introduce participants to company data located on an intranet site
Timing	Five to ten minutes

Design Considerations and Exercise Set-Up

- Consider a new hire orientation program where you want to introduce participants to company content located on the corporate intranet.
    - Identify key content items located on the corporate intranet.
    - Map out the order in which you would like the content to be presented.
    - List the URLs in the leader guide.
- Key URLs and content should be referenced in the participant guide.

Trainer Instructions

- Using the synchronized web browser, bring participants to the corporate intranet site.
- Lead participants through the key URLs, commenting on key points.
- Refer participants to the participant guide for additional information.

Producer Instructions

The producer can assist by:

- Typing site addresses into the URL locator.

Participant Instructions

Directions to participants should be concise and easy to understand. Verbally instruct participants on what they will be doing. Consider including exercise instructions in the participant guide.

- Observe and ask questions when appropriate.

Exercise Notes and Variations

- You can make this into a scavenger hunt exercise by allowing participants to browse the website on their own and answer questions in their participant guides.

How can YOU use this exercise, or a variation, in your program?

9

Other Tools to Support Your Synchronous Programs

This book has covered the major collaboration tools available in the synchronous classroom, including whiteboards, chat, breakout rooms, application sharing, and synchronized web browsing.

This chapter will be a little different. Instead of exploring one major tool in detail, we will investigate ancillary tools and techniques that can be used to help create and support your collaborative exercises. We also attempt to debunk some "myths" about the perceived collaborative values of some of these features. The tools we will review are

- Audio discussions
- Live video
- Polling and feedback
- Discussion boards

Creating Synchronous Discussions

The trainer's voice is perhaps the most important content delivery method available in a synchronous classroom. The less interesting or effective the trainer's voice is, the higher the chances are that the participants will be disengaged. (The "Best Practices" list later in this section provides tips for increasing the effectiveness of a trainer's voice.) This is because voice is the only human connection in the synchronous classroom. Without it, participants may be left feeling as if they are communicating with a "ghost in the machine." (See Figure 9.1.) You'll notice that clear audio instructions and discussions are critical to the exercises illustrated in Chapters 4 through 8.

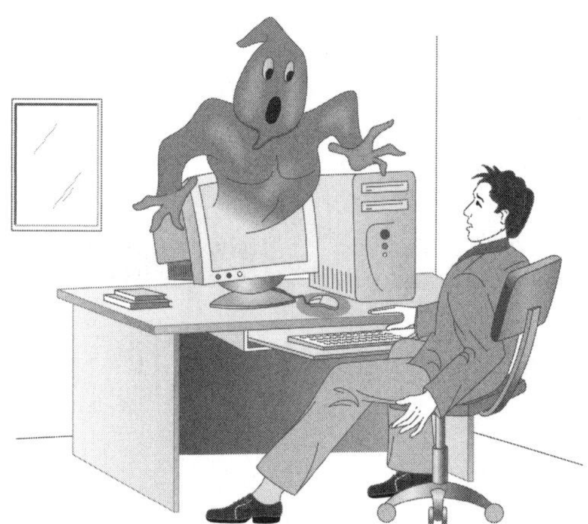

FIGURE 9.1 "Ghost in the Machine."

Adding the ability to hear other participants adds another level of potential engagement. Every time the participant is presented with another voice, the opportunity exists to re-engage him or her. Discussion, a combination of everyone's voices, is one of the most effective ways to enhance collaborative exercises. Conversely, the lack of that discussion is the best way to minimize a participant's interest in collaboration in a synchronous environment.

One-way or two-way audio is available in most synchronous packages, and each vendor handles the technology a little differently. Audio can be delivered via the Internet (VoIP) or by a phone bridge (audioconferencing). When VoIP is used, sending audio is often initiated by pressing the <Crtl> key on your keyboard.

Some organizations opt not to utilize the VoIP. For various reasons, they find audioconferencing to be a better choice for their organizations.

Whatever option is implemented, all organizations want the quality of the voice to be high, the bandwidth delay to be low, and the technology to be easy to use.

Best Practices and Techniques

Use the audio as you would in a traditional classroom—lectures, group discussions, and Q&A sessions are all effective in a synchronous classroom once the facilitation techniques have been mastered.

Trainers will need to adjust their language to accommodate the new environment, and these language adjustments should be reflected in the script. Language has to be very specific. For example, the trainer can no longer say things like, "Anybody ready for a break?" Instead, he or she must say, "If you are ready for a break, please click 'YES'; if not, click 'NO.'"

Here are some tips to help trainers manage synchronous discussions. (Designers should make sure these tips are reflected in leader guides to remind the trainer to use them.)

- Ensure maximum Internet audio quality by encouraging participants to use the audio wizard (a tool built into the synchronous classroom that helps the participant to set volume and speaker settings).
- Pace your lectures. Delivering content at an effective pace is critical to a trainer's success. Trainers are accustomed to relying on eye contact and the body language of participants to ascertain the appropriate pace for a lecture. If participants look bored, trainers speed up the program. If there are a lot of questioning or confused faces, trainers slow down. Because of the lack of these cues, there is a tendency for trainers to talk too quickly. Trainers should take breaths, stop to review the screen for feedback (text messages, raised hands, and so on), and give participants an opportunity to process and respond.
- Don't read off the screen. Even if the main points are bulleted on your slides, use your own words, anecdotes, and emphasis to explain the points. If you seem to be just reading what is written, participants will wonder why they couldn't just review the slides and may decide the time spent in the event isn't worthwhile.
- Change your inflections. When trying to emphasize an important point, strengthen your voice. Allow your voice to express your emotions, convictions, and opinions. Just as in a traditional environment, participants will tend to be more interested in what you have to say if you sound as though YOU are interested in what you have to say.
- Call on people using their names. This gives participants something to listen for and encourages them to pay attention.
- Plan to use multiple voices whenever possible. If a participant has become distracted, hearing a different voice might be just the inducement he or she needs to become re-engaged. Experts, assistant trainers, and participants all have voices to lend to the discussion.
- Minimize references to the technology. When you say things like, "I see you have your hand up; do you have a question?" it sounds awkward. Try, "Mary, what is your question?" Also avoid saying things like, "Please wait while I launch an application." Instead, assign a chat exercise or something else to engage participants while you are setting up your exercises.

- While group collaboration is an important goal, it is sometimes equally important to use a serial approach and to let each individual with an opinion have his or her say. For example, you may want to include individual participant experiences to illustrate an instructional point. When two-way audio is available, use "round robin" techniques to facilitate this. To make conversation seem more natural and move more quickly, encourage some "round robin" discussions. For example, consider adapting the following dialog:

  "John, please give us your opinion. Mary, as soon as he is finished it will be your turn to share. Then Scott, Lynn, Liz, and Ellen. You don't need to wait for me to call on you—just go ahead and speak."

Best Practices for Alternate Audio Techniques

Sometimes audioconferencing and one-way audio present special issues. Implementing these best practices will help to ensure effective discussions.

Audioconferencing Best Practices

- Participants should use the "MUTE" button so the extraneous noise is not transmitted to the rest of the class.
- Avoid putting the call on "HOLD." Often, the "music on hold" feature may kick on and disrupt the class until that person returns.
- Participants should still raise their virtual hands when they have questions and wait for the trainer to call on them unless an open discussion is called.
- Participants should identify themselves before speaking.
- If participants are using a handset or cell phone, they must make sure batteries are fully charged.
- Bad cell phone connections can be very distracting. You may need to ask participants with bad connections not to talk.

One-Way Internet Audio Best Practices

- Encourage chat interactions to make up for the lack of audio.
- Continue to call on participants by name, but while they are answering your questions in the chat area, continue with your discussion. This will take some planning so the program doesn't seem disjointed.
- There is a tendency to lecture when participants can't verbally communicate. Use chat and whiteboard techniques to encourage continuous collaboration and communication.

Video

One-way or two-way video is offered by more sophisticated synchronous packages. This is a very technology-intensive feature, which often limits its use to participants using broadband connections. (An exception is the use of streaming media in one-way video configurations, which can be effectively fed to participants with connections as slow as 56 Kbps.)

While many buyers insist on this feature being available in their synchronous classroom platform, because of technical and bandwidth constraints, it is not often used in training programs.

FIGURE 9.2 Live Video.

Instructional Uses

One of the side-effects of implementing a synchronous classroom is the realization by trainers that their physical presence is not critical to instruction. This often makes trainers uncomfortable and makes many concerned that their jobs are in peril. (Of course, this is not the case! The synchronous classroom requires effective, dynamic trainers with an updated presentation skill set.)

(*Note:* For more information on the roles of the online trainer and assistant trainer, see Chapter 2 of *The Synchronous Trainer's Survival Guide*.)

Live video is often seen as a way to re-introduce the trainer's physical presence into the virtual classroom.

In my opinion, live video should be used judiciously. Using live video throughout an entire session can distract from the content and provide additional technological challenges. Additionally, by focusing so closely on the trainer's face, you may reduce the perceived opportunities for participant collaboration.

Eventually, participants and trainers alike will have nearly ubiquitous access to the bandwidth, hardware, and software required to effectively stream quality live video from their desktops. When that occurs, instructional designers will have more exercise and design options for including multiple video streams. For example, if, during a live event, participants can work in pairs using a combination of voice and video (perhaps in breakout rooms) they may be able to achieve a more collaborative working relationship than they can now by using voice or chat. We may also be able to evaluate skills that include physical presence.

One way to collaboratively use live video is to implement it during Q&A portions of a program. Have an off-camera moderator manage participants' questions and have the expert answer by looking directly into the camera. This may give the answers more of a personal feel and encourage more attention. Turn the camera off when group discussion resumes.

If face-to-face interactions are critical, consider using a traditional classroom approach instead. Or record video and distribute before the session using the Internet, videotape, or CD-ROM. If everyone can't see the video, consider not using it all. It may be frustrating for participants who feel they are not getting the "full" experience.

Variations and Considerations

Here are some questions you should ask your vendor before designing exercises.

- *What are the hardware and software requirements?* This has to be managed and tested long before the event. Ask your vendor to provide detailed specifications and test with participants representing your target audience.
- *Does video have to be sent to everyone?* Some platforms recognize users with dial-up connections and automatically suppress video to those users or send out fewer "frames per second."

- *Is there any way to see live video of the participants?* Some synchronous software packages offer live video of participants who have the specified hardware. Whenever a participant is speaking, his or her video data is streamed out to the rest of the class. Again, ask your vendor for detailed specifications.

Polling and Feedback

Various devices have been built into synchronous platforms to compensate for the loss of eye contact and body language.

Some varieties of survey, polling, and feedback tools are available in all platforms. They help you to get a quick check on the pulse of the class and allow the participants to apprise the trainer on the pace and clarity of the content. (See Figure 9.3.)

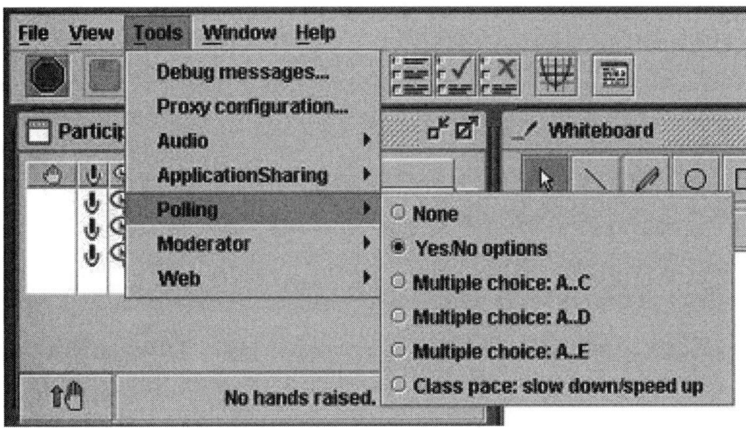

FIGURE 9.3 Polling and Feedback.

Instructional Uses

Training professionals new to the synchronous classroom often use polling devices as a way to try to engage students and encourage collaboration. Those with more experience have learned that having a participant click on a button might ensure that participants are still sitting in front of the computer, but it doesn't mean that they are actually engaged, learning, or ready to collaborate.

Here are some basic ideas to help you start using polling and feedback devices. Notice that they are not collaboration techniques per se, but they can be incorporated into whiteboard, chat, and other types of more collaborative exercises. You should do your best to design even simple feedback interactions for your program and not rely entirely on ad hoc audience polling.

- Use surveys and polls to determine whether the participants understand the material and to keep them tuned in to the lesson.
- Use surveys to transition to a new topic by asking questions about the new topic and then commenting on the results.
- Create icebreakers and introductory exercises by polling the audience.
- Share results with the class to foster a sense of community.
- Asking participants to provide feedback can be a good re-engagement technique if the audience is not participating.
- Anonymous feedback allows participants to be honest without worrying about repercussions.

If you are not comfortable with receiving and responding to continual feedback, you might introduce this feature slowly.

Variations and Considerations

Here are some questions you should ask your vendor before designing exercises that incorporate feedback.

- What survey and/or polling tools are available with the platform?
- Can the results be shared with the class?
- Can questions be created spontaneously?
- Is the feedback anonymous/confidential?

Discussion Boards

A discussion board (Figure 9.4) is an asynchronous feature that allows participants to post messages and replies to messages by topic. (Discussion boards are asynchronous tools because participants do not use them in real time.)

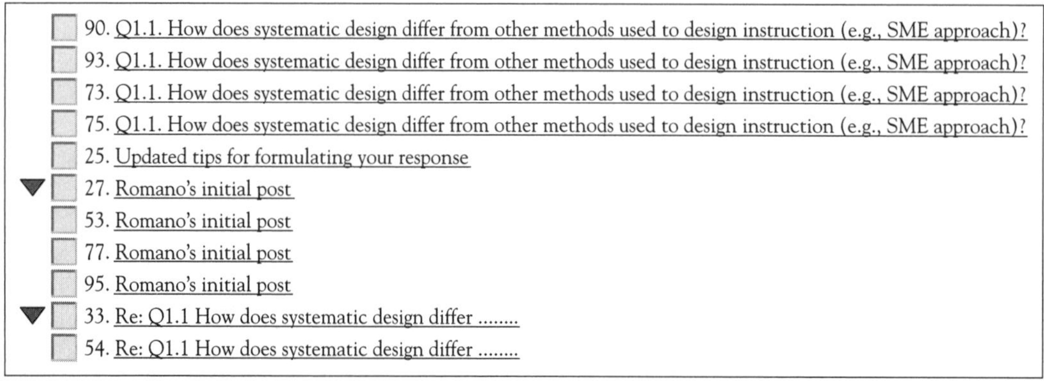

FIGURE 9.4 Discussion Boards.

While a discussion board is an asynchronous feature, it is often bundled with synchronous packages. Often, classes that include both asynchronous activities, such as a discussion board, and short synchronous online sessions are more effective than those using just one delivery method because they appeal to participants who excel in each environment.

Discussion boards support a collaborative learning environment by providing an avenue to tie synchronous events together and by giving participants a space in which to collaborate between the live events.

Instructional Uses

Here are some basic ideas to help you start using discussion boards to support collaboration before, in-between, and after your live synchronous events.

- Use discussion boards to post class information, frequently asked questions, pre- or post-session assignments, subject-matter expert insights, or other information relevant to the synchronous session.
- For multi-session classes, encourage participants to use the discussion boards for knowledge sharing and community building. You'll need to stay involved to make sure this is successful.
- Use the same discussion board area for different groups taking the same class. This will allow participants to learn from, and perhaps interact with, participants who have already completed the program. It is the potential start for a learning community around the topic.

Variations and Considerations

Here are some questions you should ask your vendor before designing exercises.

- *Is a discussion board available with my synchronous platform?* If your software does not have a discussion board, you can consider a third-party product like Blackboard™ (www.blackboard.com) or WebCT™ (www.webct.com).
- *Is the discussion board available during class?* If so, you can access homework responses or comment on the activity.
- *Can multiple groups of participants access the same discussion board?* If each offering of a course forces the use of a new discussion board, you may need to find other ways for multiple classes to cross-collaborate.

In Closing

There are many, many steps involved in creating a successful synchronous program. Effective learning environments have to be established, trainers must be ready to teach, and participants must be ready to learn. But even if all of these factors are in place, you are not guaranteed success. Synchronous programs have to be designed to maximize interaction and collaboration between participants. Collaboration is more than a "click here if you agree" phenomenon. Collaboration occurs when the trainer is able to facilitate exercises that allow participants to express themselves and prove their knowledge.

I hope that this book, *Live and Online! Tips, Techniques, and Ready-to-Use Activities for the Virtual Classroom*, has provided you with a framework that allows your trainers to establish a collaborative relationship with their participants.

Good luck and I'll see you online!

APPENDIX A

Synchronous Classroom Vendors

The following vendors provide a synchronous virtual classroom. They all contain some combination of synchronous classroom features, as described in Appendix B.

Company Name:	Centra
Product:	CentraOne
Website:	www.centra.com
City:	Lexington
State:	MA
phone:	781-861-7000
email:	info@centra.com

Company Name:	EDT Learning
Product:	LearnLinc
Website:	www.edtlearning.com
City:	Phoenix
State:	AZ
phone:	602-952-1200
email:	inquiry@edtlearning.com

Company Name:	Elluminate
Product:	vClass
Website:	www.elluminate.com
City:	Pompano Beach
State:	FL
phone:	954-781-7958
email:	sales@elluminate.com

Company Name:	HorizonLive
Product:	HorizonLive
Website:	www.horizonlive.com
City:	New York
State:	NY
phone:	212-533-1775
email:	info@horizonlive.com

Company Name:	IBM Lotus Software
Product:	Lotus Virtual Classroom
Website:	www.lotus.com
City:	White Plains
State:	NY
phone:	800-IBM-4YOU (800-426-4968)
email:	ibm_direct@vnet.ibm.com

Company Name:	Interwise
Product:	Enterprise Communication Platform
Website:	www.interwise.com
City:	Cambridge

State: MA

phone: 617-475-2200

email: Generic email not available

Company Name: Microsoft

Product Name: NetMeeting

Website: www.microsoft.com/windows/netmeeting/

City: Redmond

State: WA

phone: Generic phone not available

email: Generic email not available

Company: Microsoft

Product: Microsoft Office Live Meeting

Website: www.placeware.com

City: Mountain View

State: CA

phone: 888-526-6170

email: marketing@placeware.com

Company: Raindance Communications

Product: Raindance Web Conferencing

Website: www.raindance.com

City: Louisville

State: CO

phone: 800-878-7326

email: sales@raindance.com

Company Name:	WebEx Communications
Product:	WebEx
Website:	www.webex.com
City:	San Jose
State:	CA
phone:	408-435-7000
email:	info@webex.com

APPENDIX B

Synchronous Features Table

SYNCHRONOUS FEATURE: AUDIO

One-way or two-way audio is available in most synchronous packages. Audio can be delivered via the Internet (VOIP) or by a phone bridge (audioconferencing). When VOIP is used, sending audio is often initiated by pressing the <Crtl> key on your keyboard.

Some organizations opt not to utilize the VOIP. For various reasons, they find audioconferencing to be a better choice for their organizations.

USES

- The trainer's voice is perhaps the most important content delivery method available in a synchronous classroom.
- Use the audio as you would in a traditional classroom—lectures, group discussions, and Q&A sessions are all effective in a synchronous classroom once the facilitation techniques have been mastered.

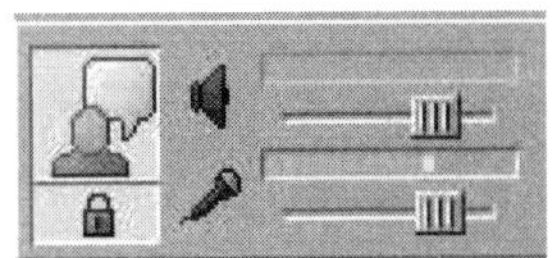

Centra Audio Controls

CONSIDERATIONS

- What type of audio (full-duplex, half-duplex, telephone conferencing) is available?
- Does the software have some kind of "wizard" to test audio settings?

SYNCHRONOUS FEATURE: CHAT

Text-based chat allows the participants and trainer to communicate with one another through text messaging. Private messaging allows participants to signal difficulties without disrupting a session.

Often, chat discussions (or transcripts) can be saved as text files and used after the event is over.

USES

- Participants who are more reserved are often more likely to interact when text chat options are available.
- Questions can be "parked" to be answered later—either during or after the class session.
- You can conduct brainstorming sessions in the chat room.
- If you have a technical support person online, he or she can monitor the chat to identify and fix technical problems without interrupting the class. If you happen to be using a subject-matter expert, he or she can monitor a classroom in order to answer content-related questions that may be out of the scope of the current lecture or activity.
- Independent or group exercise instructions can be pasted from a word processor into a chat area for participants to review during an exercise.
- Some software platforms offer group chat areas, while others have features that more closely resemble an Instant Messenger function (sometimes called "Notes").

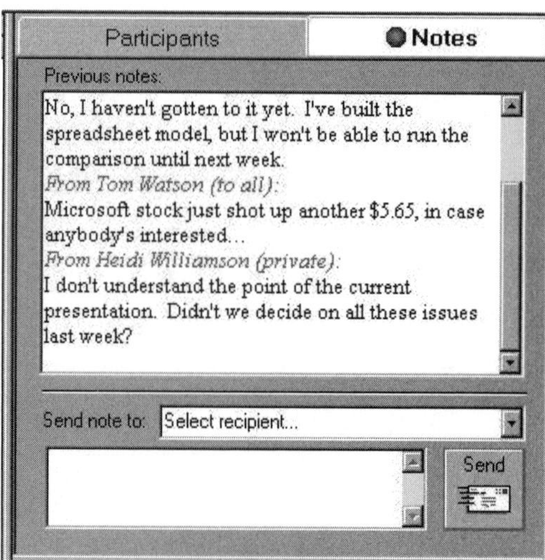

Sample "Notes" Area

CONSIDERATIONS

- Is full group chat available?
- Is private messaging to the trainer/assistant trainer available?
- Is private messaging between participants allowed?
- Can a transcript of chat conversations be saved?
- Does the transcript include private messaging?

SYNCHRONOUS FEATURE: BREAKOUT ROOMS

This feature allows small groups to meet and share information during a larger synchronous session.

USES

- Breakout rooms are ideal for training sessions in which teams or groups can share specific content.
- Participants can be assigned to individual breakout rooms to complete a self-paced exercise or assessment.

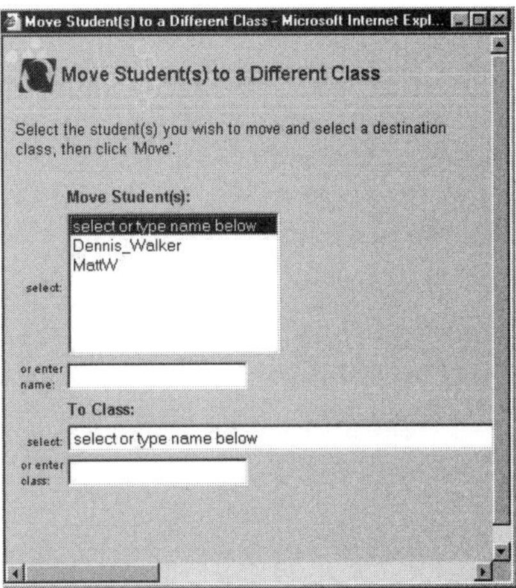

HorizonLive Breakout Dialog

- Team competitions can be conducted.
- You can work with groups or individuals on an as-needed basis.
- Different groups can work with different content or on different exercises.
- If there are varying levels of expertise in a class, a program can be divided and different trainers can moderate the breakout rooms.
- Breakout room instructions need to be very clear, since the trainer is not always available.

CONSIDERATIONS

- What features (whiteboards, application sharing, and so forth) are available in the breakout rooms?
- Can participants be pre-assigned to a particular room?
- Can participants be moved from room to room during an activity?
- Can materials (whiteboards and other items) created in breakout rooms be shared when the large group is reconvened?

SYNCHRONOUS FEATURE: WHITEBOARDS

- Roughly the synchronous equivalent of a traditional flip chart, whiteboards allow trainers and participants to post ideas. The primary difference is that many whiteboards allow multiple people to write at the same time.
- Images can be placed on prepared whiteboards (often in the form of PowerPoint™ slides) ahead of time or pasted during the session.

Some synchronous applications allow users to take a "snapshot" of a part of an application and paste that snapshot to the whiteboard for annotation. Some whiteboards are "object-oriented," which means each individual drawing can be moved or deleted.

USES

- Use the whiteboard for anything you would use a flip chart or marker board for in a traditional classroom setting. For example, you can capture expectations at the beginning of a class and revisit them at the end of a program.

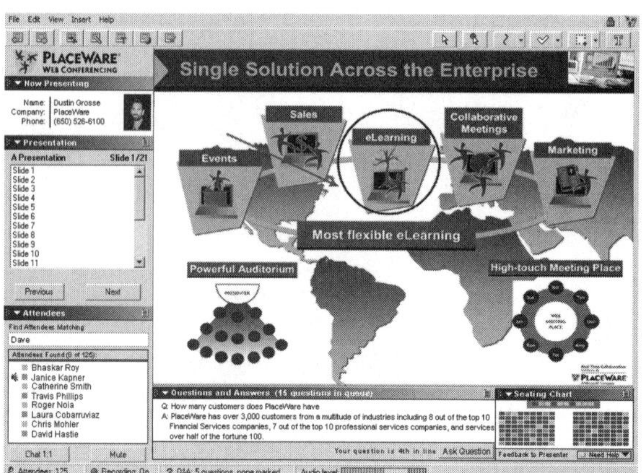

PlaceWare, Inc.—Full Console and Slide Controls

- Content changes and additions can be captured and used to revise the program.
- You can capture participants' ideas in flip-chart style.
- Whiteboards can often be archived for reuse in asynchronous applications or emailed to class participants.
- Content can be highlighted as it is discussed, which makes lectures more meaningful.
- Icebreakers and games can also be created using the whiteboard.

CONSIDERATIONS

- Can you save whiteboards created during the event?
- Can graphics be pasted or imported to the whiteboard?
- How many people can write on the whiteboard at once?
- If you return to a slide that you have written on, will the comments still be there?
- What tools are available for whiteboard drawing?
- Can drawing and graphics be moved once they are on the whiteboard?

SYNCHRONOUS FEATURE: SURVEYS/POLLS/FEEDBACK/ HANDRAISING/PACING/COMPREHENSION

Various devices have been built into synchronous platforms to compensate for the loss of eye contact and body language.

A variety of survey, polling, and feedback tools are available in all platforms. They help you to get a quick check on the pulse of the class and allow the participants to appraise the trainer on the pace and clarity of the content.

USES

- Use surveys and polls to determine whether the participants understand the material and to keep them tuned in to the lesson.
- Use surveys to transition to a new topic by asking questions about the new topic and then commenting on the results.
- Create icebreakers and introductory exercises by polling the audience.
- Share results with the class to foster a sense of community.

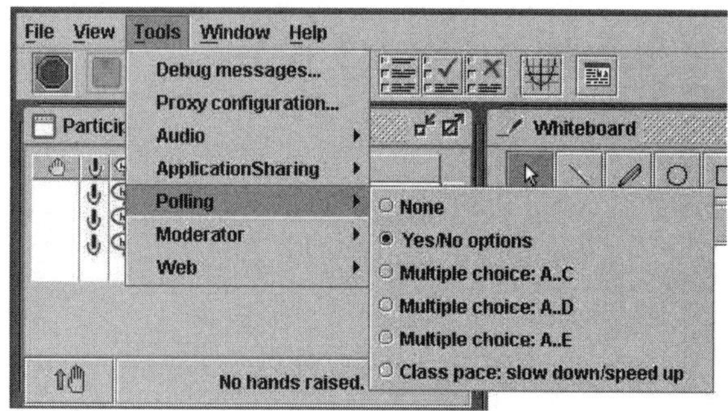

vClass Polling Menu

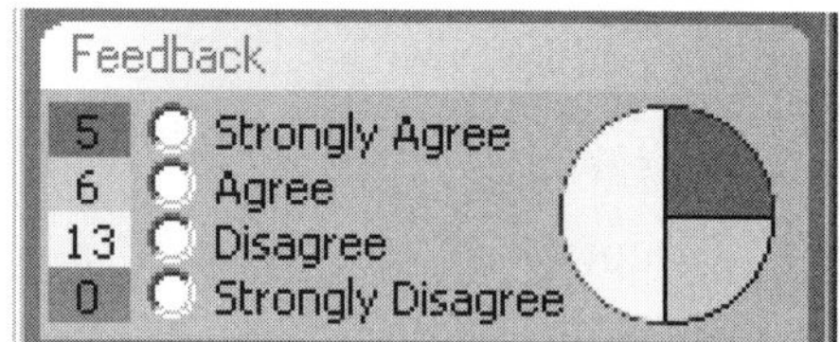

Instructor Feedback Results in LearnLinc

- Asking participants to provide feedback can be a good reengagement technique if the audience is not participating.
- Anonymous feedback allows participants to be honest without worrying about repercussions.
- If you are not comfortable with receiving and responding to continual feedback, you might introduce this feature slowly.

CONSIDERATIONS

- What survey and/or polling tools are available with the platform?
- Can the results be shared with the class?
- Can questions be created spontaneously?
- Is the feedback anonymous/confidential?

SYNCHRONOUS FEATURE: TESTING/EVALUATION

This feature allows the trainer to conduct pre-session and post-session assessments and tests, the results of which can be automatically tabulated and saved.

USES

- Use this feature to assess your participants' comprehension and retention.

- If these built-in solutions aren't robust enough, savvy users can create assessments in HTML and post them to participants using the application window. Or participants can be instructed to use commercial web-based assessment tools like QuestionMark™ (www.questionmark.com) and Zoomerang™ (www.zoomerang.com).

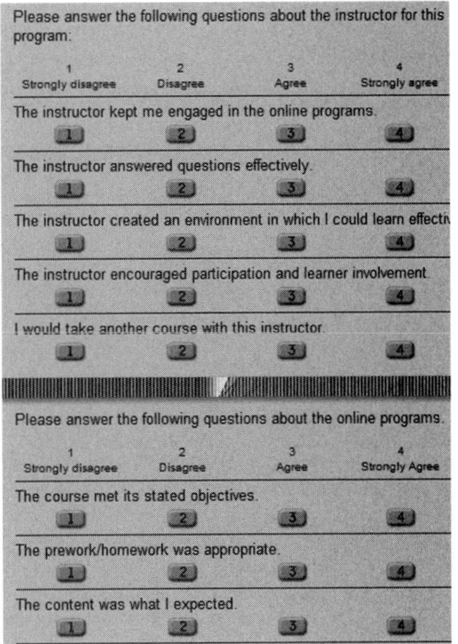

Please answer the following questions about the instructor for this program:

1 Strongly disagree | 2 Disagree | 3 Agree | 4 Strongly agree

The instructor kept me engaged in the online programs.
1 2 3 4

The instructor answered questions effectively.
1 2 3 4

The instructor created an environment in which I could learn effecti
1 2 3 4

The instructor encouraged participation and learner involvement.
1 2 3 4

I would take another course with this instructor.
1 2 3 4

Please answer the following questions about the online programs.

1 Strongly disagree | 2 Disagree | 3 Agree | 4 Strongly Agree

The course met its stated objectives.
1 2 3 4

The prework/homework was appropriate.
1 2 3 4

The content was what I expected.
1 2 3 4

Sample Course Evaluation

CONSIDERATIONS

- How are evaluation and testing results reported?
- How are results saved?

SYNCHRONOUS FEATURE: LIVE VIDEO

One-way or two-way video is offered by more sophisticated synchronous packages.

This is a very technology-intensive feature, which often limits its use to participants using broadband connections. (An exception is the use of streaming media in one-way video configurations, which can be fed to participants with connections as slow as 56 Kbps.)

Some platforms recognize users with dial-up connections and automatically suppress video to those users or send out fewer "frames per second."

USES

- You can use the video to look directly into the camera for live Q&A sessions.
- Using live video throughout a session can be very distracting; you should use it judiciously. If face-to-face interactions are critical, consider using a traditional classroom approach instead. Or record video and distribute before the session using the Internet, videotape, or CD-ROM.

LearnLinc's Video Viewer

CONSIDERATIONS

- What are the hardware and software requirements for live video?

SYNCHRONOUS FEATURE: DISCUSSION BOARDS

A discussion board is an asynchronous feature that allows participants to post messages and replies to messages by topic. Discussion boards are different from chat in that they are not real-time.

While a discussion board is an asynchronous feature, it is often bundled with synchronous packages.

If your software does not have a discussion board, you can consider a third-party product like Blackboard™ (www.blackboard.com) or WebCT™ (www.webtct.com).

USES

- Use discussion boards to post class information, FAQs, pre-session or post-session assignments, subject-matter expert insights, or other information relevant to the synchronous session.

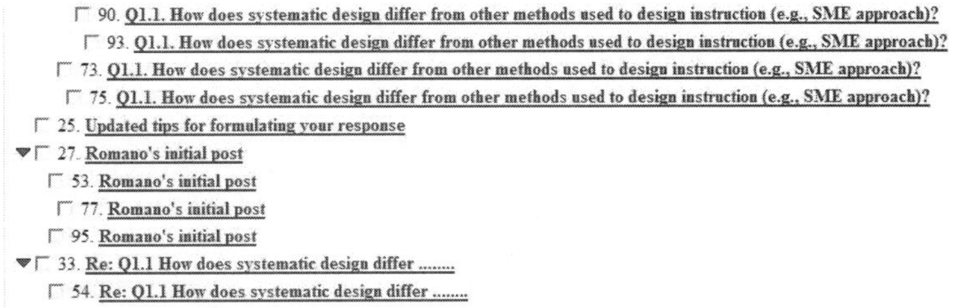

90. Q1.1. How does systematic design differ from other methods used to design instruction (e.g., SME approach)?
93. Q1.1. How does systematic design differ from other methods used to design instruction (e.g., SME approach)?
73. Q1.1. How does systematic design differ from other methods used to design instruction (e.g., SME approach)?
75. Q1.1. How does systematic design differ from other methods used to design instruction (e.g., SME approach)?
25. Updated tips for formulating your response
27. Romano's initial post
53. Romano's initial post
77. Romano's initial post
95. Romano's initial post
33. Re: Q1.1 How does systematic design differ ....
54. Re: Q1.1 How does systematic design differ ....

Sample Threaded Discussion

- For multi-session classes, encourage participants to use the discussion boards for knowledge sharing and community building. You'll need to stay involved to make sure this is successful.
- Often, classes that include such asynchronous activities as discussion boards and short synchronous online sessions are more effective than using just one delivery method.

CONSIDERATIONS

- Are discussion boards available during class?

SYNCHRONOUS FEATURE: APPLICATION SHARING

This feature allows the trainer to share software applications (such as spreadsheets) with participants.

There are many varieties of this feature, ranging from "view only" on the participants' side to allowing participants to actually interact with applications shared by the trainer or by other participants.

USES

- Use application sharing to demonstrate software features.
- Small groups can collaborate by sharing common office software packages.
- Individuals can walk through software applications with which they are having difficulty.
- Participants can use shared applications in breakout rooms. There, you can also assist individuals with assigned exercises.

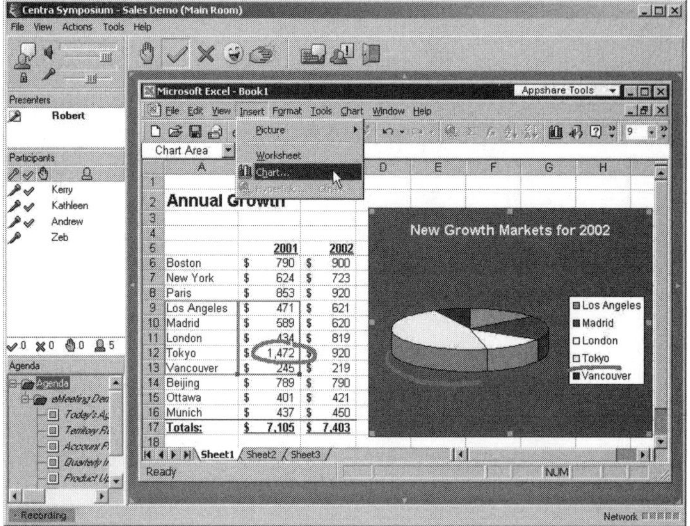

Application Sharing in Centra Symposium (Student View)

CONSIDERATIONS

- What types of applications can be shared?
- What are the bandwidth requirements for application sharing?
- Can participants interact with the application or just view it?

SYNCHRONOUS FEATURE: SYNCHRONIZED WEB BROWSING

This feature allows the trainer or participants to bring the class to an Internet site or corporate intranet.

Often, you can use this feature to run short, self-paced exercises as part of a synchronous session.

USES

- Instead of recreating content that already exists, you can use the Internet or corporate intranet as a content source.
- Participants can share related content by your leading the class to a website.
- Independent exercises can be initiated for the entire group—including web-enabled, self-paced exercises created in multimedia applications.
- Last-minute content can be added to an existing program by placing it on the web.

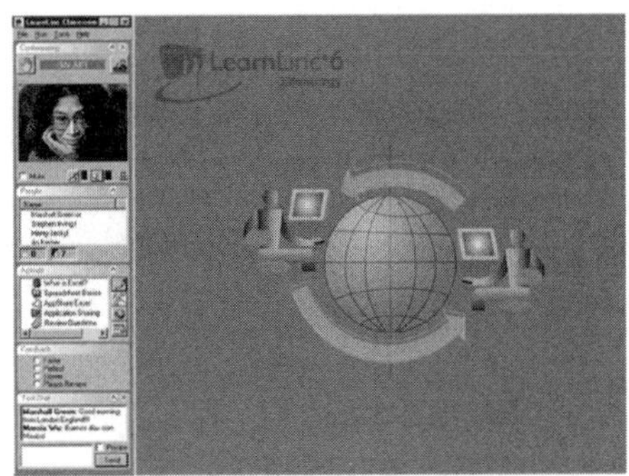

LearnLinc's Synchronized Web Browser

CONSIDERATIONS

- Can a participant bring the class to a website?
- Can bookmarks be created prior to class to speed navigation?
- Does this feature require a specific browser?
- Are hyperlinks available to individual participants?

SYNCHRONOUS FEATURE: RECORD AND PLAYBACK

This feature allows individuals to record synchronous events and play them back later.

Often, parts of recordings can be edited into synchronous sessions or entire recordings can be "cleaned up" for on-demand viewing.

This feature helps individuals who miss sessions and allows for quick creation of asynchronous training content.

USES

- You can use the record/playback feature to practice and review the participants' and the trainer's performances.
- You can preview existing programs to review content.
- Participants can use recordings to preview or review course materials.
- Participants who miss one session of a multi-session program need not miss the content.
- This is a relatively inexpensive way to create self-paced, "videotaped" classes.
- This feature is a very efficient way to prep new trainers.
- Be sure to tell participants they are being recorded! Often, there is an indicator on the screen to act as a reminder.

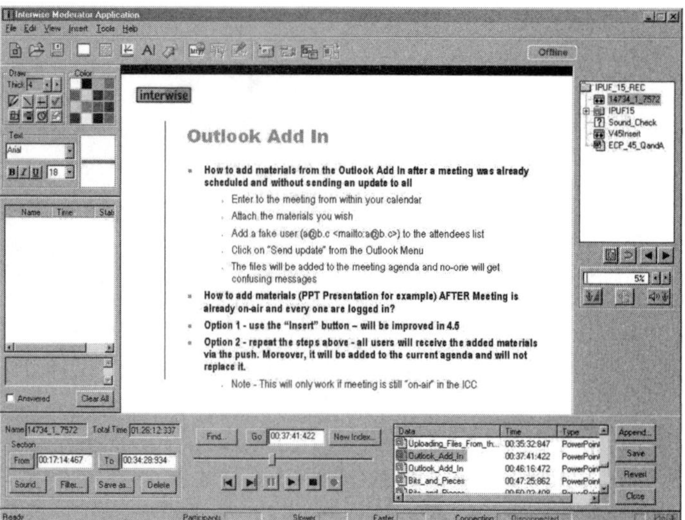

Interwise Recording Editor

CONSIDERATIONS

- Is special software required to view the recordings?
- Can recordings be viewed while not connected to the Internet?
- Can trainers stop the recorder and start it up again in the same session?

SYNCHRONOUS FEATURE: ASSISTANT TRAINER

Feature that allows a second individual to assist the trainer with some of the facilitation tasks. Some programs allow for multiple assistants.

Assistant trainers do not need to be in the same location as the trainer, but they can still use an "instructor" version of the synchronous application to conduct various tasks—from dealing with technical support issues to helping with the content.

USES

- If your class requires a subject-matter expert in the delivery, he or she can help in the assistant trainer role by answering questions and providing lecture assistance.
- The assistant trainer role is perfect for a trainer-in-training. The assistant trainer can interact as a participant and assist you at the same time.
- If you have a special guest trainer who doesn't know how to manage the synchronous technology, you can manage the technology while the guest, acting as the assistant, leads the discussion.

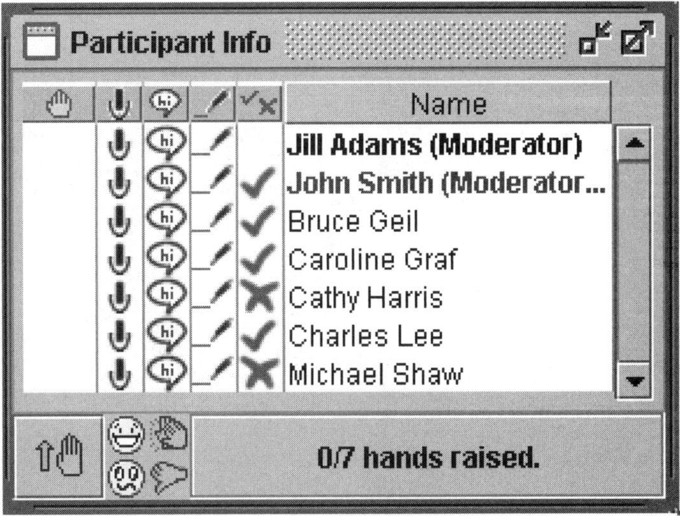

In vClass the Assistant Trainer Is Identified by the Word "Moderator"

CONSIDERATIONS

- What can a lead trainer do that an assistant trainer cannot do (create breakout rooms, launch applications, and so forth)?
- Do assistants need to be identified ahead of time, or can individuals be "promoted" during the live event?

SYNCHRONOUS FEATURE: CONTENT WINDOWS

Content windows are used to display content in HTML, PowerPoint® or other web-ready media.

PowerPoint is the most popular content creation tool. When the slides are loaded into some synchronous platforms, the slides may become backgrounds for whiteboards.

USES

- Remember that synchronous classrooms are a very visual medium. What you show in the content windows needs to be relevant and engaging.
- Don't plan to read the content on your screen verbatim. If that's the nature of the content, consider an asynchronous or self-paced delivery instead.
- Use multimedia when it makes sense—not just because you can. Remember that every time you add a new technology, you are also adding a potential technical obstacle.
- Some software packages allow you to use pre-created content as whiteboard backgrounds. This can be a very effective engagement tool.

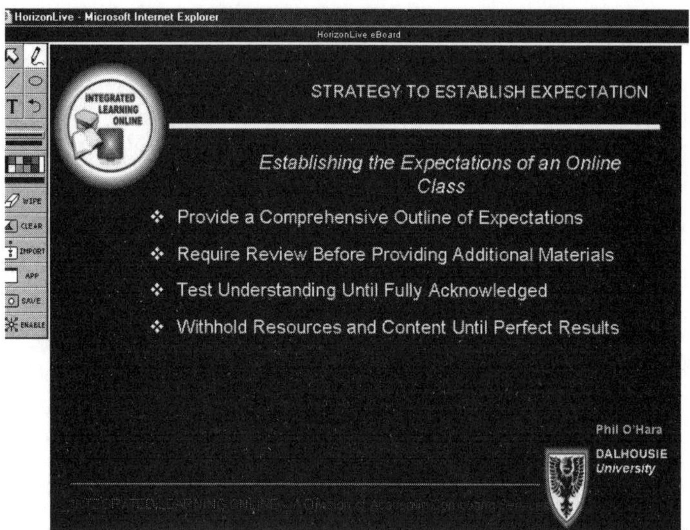

HorizonLive's Content Window "eBoard"

CONSIDERATIONS

- Can content be added during the live event?
- How are plug-ins managed?
- What file formats can be used?
- Are web and/or PowerPoint animations viewable?
- Can you write on top of animated content?

APPENDIX C

Synchronous Considerations Checklist

Use this checklist to document the specifics of your particular synchronous training platform. Bring it to synchronous software training and ask your trainer, or spend the time to investigate on your own.

Software Platform: ______________________________

Version: ___________________

AUDIO CONSIDERATIONS | NOTES

- What type of audio (full-duplex, half-duplex, telephone conferencing) is available?
- Does the software have some kind of "wizard" to test audio settings?

CHAT CONSIDERATIONS | NOTES

- Is full group chat available?
- Is private messaging to the trainer/assistant trainer available?
- Is private messaging between participants allowed?
- Can a transcript of chat conversations be saved?

- Does the transcript include private messaging?

BREAKOUT ROOM CONSIDERATIONS	NOTES
• What features (application sharing, and so forth) are available in the breakout rooms? • Can participants be pre-assigned to a particular room? • Can participants be moved from room to room during an activity? • Can materials (whiteboards and so on) created in breakout rooms be shared when the large group is reconvened?	

WHITEBOARD CONSIDERATIONS	NOTES
• Can you save whiteboards created during the event? • Can graphics be pasted or imported to the whiteboard? • How many people can write on the whiteboard at once? • If you return to a slide that you have written on, will the comments still be there? • What tools are available for whiteboard drawing? • Can drawing and graphics be moved once they are on the whiteboard?	

SURVEYS/POLLS/FEEDBACK/ HAND RAISING/PACING/ COMPREHENSION CONSIDERATIONS	NOTES
• What survey and/or polling tools are available with the platform? • Can the results be shared with the class? • Can questions be created spontaneously?	

- Is the feedback anonymous/confidential?

Testing and Evaluation Considerations	Notes
• How are evaluation and testing results reported? • How are results saved?	

Live Video Considerations	Notes
• What are the hardware and software requirements for live video?	

Discussion Board Considerations	Notes
• Are discussion boards available during class?	

Application Sharing Considerations	Notes
• What types of applications can be shared? • What are the bandwidth requirements for application sharing? • Can participants interact with the application or just view it?	

Synchronized Web Browsing Considerations	Notes
• Can a participant bring the class to a website? • Can bookmarks be created prior to class to speed navigation? • Does this feature require a specific browser? • Are hyperlinks available to individual participants?	

Record/Playback Considerations	Notes
• Is special software required to view the recordings? • Can recordings be viewed while not connected to the Internet? • Can trainers stop the recorder and start it up again in the same session?	

Assistant Trainer Considerations	Notes
• What can a lead trainer do that an assistant trainer cannot do (for example, create breakout rooms, launch applications)? • Do assistants have to be identified ahead of time, or can individuals be "promoted" during the live event?	

Content Windows Considerations	Notes
• Can content be added during the live event? • How are plug-ins managed? • What file formats can be used? • Are web and/or PowerPoint™ animations viewable? • Can you write on top of animated content?	

Miscellaneous Feature Considerations	Notes

Miscellaneous Feature Considerations	Notes

APPENDIX D

Interactivity Plan

When creating a design plan for a live online learning session, the instructional designer must keep the needs of many different individuals in mind. Since so many individuals are new to the medium, it is helpful to communicate ideas in a format that works for everyone, including:

1. **The Subject-Matter Expert,** who needs to be able to determine that content is being communicated effectively.
2. **The Media Producer,** who needs to understand the context of the media he or she is producing.
3. **The Trainer,** who needs to have a script and understand how the technology is being used in context with the content.
4. **The Producer,** who needs to have a big picture view and understand his or her role in supporting the trainer and participants.
5. **The Participants,** who need materials that complement the training program, and resources to extend the learning beyond the live event.

It can be a challenge to create a plan that meets the needs of all these individuals. One method is to create an Interactivity Plan, a table that contains the following columns:

- Step
- Time Reference (cumulative/step)
- Topic
- Objective
- Instructional Method

- Screen Design/Additional Media Notes
- Choreography/Script
- Production Notes/Development Questions

This tool can be a great design template for your team. The following details each component of the table.

Step. The step column looks for a number (1, 2, 3.). This identifies the point in the process. It's helpful for everyone involved because you can refer to a specific step when reviewing the design document.

Time Reference. There are two ways to track time. The first is cumulatively. For instance, at step 23, you should be 45 minutes into the program. Tracking time this way provides cues to the trainer that he or she is on track, and tells the stage director what he or she should expect during the next time block. The second way to track time is by step. For example, introductions might be step 5, and it might take 10 minutes to accomplish. You should decide up front which way of tracking time would provide the most value to your project.

Topic. This column represents the general content area you're covering during the step. For example, if you're teaching general anatomy, "Nervous System" might be an appropriate topic. The topic may be repeated for multiple steps. In this area you may want to include a "content reference." This is especially helpful if you're designing a course using an existing set of materials. It allows the team to cross-reference content easily. In the case of our anatomy class, we might reference a textbook by indicating "*Gray's Anatomy*, page 66."

Objective. The objective provides the point of the current activity. An example could be "To provide participants a definition of the nervous system." When a topic is repeated multiple times, the step objective really comes in handy.

Instructional Method. Are you using an interactive whiteboard exercise? A polling question? Lecture? The instructional method column identifies the "how."

Screen Design/Additional Media Notes. This column describes the eventual visual presentation in a text-based format. For example, you'd note here whether the instructional media is a Flash animation or a PowerPoint slide. You can also take notes about what fonts and colors you'll use.

Choreography/Script. This column identifies what the trainer needs to do (launch whiteboard, advance slide, and so forth) and what the trainer needs to say. This column is the start of your trainer guide.

Development Questions. "Where are we going to get the photos?" "Do we need a plug-in for sound?" "Maryellen will be responsible for the participant guide." These are examples of what you might place in your production notes column. It's a place that indicates that a flag or follow-up is needed. Also, as you are designing each activity, you should make a note about what participants need in front of them—not on the screen—to be successful. Do they need a calculator? PowerPoint slides? Case studies? Identify these items now so they don't get lost in the process.

This Interactivity Plan is a working document that will evolve with your project planning. It provides an at-a-glance framework of where you are and what you need to create a successful program.

After using this format, you will probably modify it to better complement your personal work style.

The following table contains an excerpt from an in-progress Interactivity Plan. (But really—a planning document is never fully complete!) It illustrates the flow for the early class activities.

A template for this plan is located on the accompanying CD.

Pre-Event Warm Up—15 Minutes Before Class Begins

Step	*Time Ref. Cum. Step*	*Topic*	*Objective*	*Instructional Method*	*Screen Design/Additional Media Notes*	*Choreography & Script*	*Development Questions*
1	—	PreEvent Welcome	To make sure participants are in the right place	NA	Welcome to "CLASS NAME"	Producer starts class and welcomes participants to the virtual classroom.	Can we develop a logo for the class?
2	—	Tech Check	To make sure they went through the Tech Check	poll	Poll: Did you do the Tech Check?	Producer conducts poll. Asks anyone who did not go through tech check to go to lobby.	
3	—	Whiteboard Review	To achieve comfort level w/whiteboard	Game—Hangman	Pre-prepared whiteboard with terms	Producer launches whiteboard and conducts hangman games.	Need 3 hangman terms for game.
4	—	Polling Review	Pre-work review—polling comfort	Game—Trivia	Various polling questions	Producer conducts polls—posts correct answers	Need up to 6 polling questions based on prework
5	—	Chat Review	Chat comfort	Game—Jeopardy type quiz show	Chat	Producer brings up Jeopardy questions in media area. Asks participants to answer in the chat room. First one to answer wins	Need up to 6 Jeopardy questions based on the prework
6	—	Technical Support	To provide technical support	Recurring theme	Message on every screen	If you need help, call tech support at: Say "Remember, if you need technical support call ___________"	What about tech support outside of the U.S.?

7	—	Audio Check	To check audio	To start to share participants' expectations for the course	• Q&A • Write question on screen • Say "raise your hand. I'll call on you in order." • Call on participants in order and ask them to say what they hope to get out of the class. NOTE: This is NOT formal introductions. However, instructor should jot down notes of what participants say about expectations in order to address some of them later when discussing course objectives.	Need to have a time limit associated with this exercise or it will be too long. Perhaps ask them for one sentence only about one key thing they hope to get out of the class.	
8	15 Min.	Transition (bullet recap—tie chunks together)	To transition from Warm Up to "Session"	Lecture/ whiteboard	Bullet points with "checkmarks"—in whiteboard	Over the last few minutes we've used the tools. . . . These are the ways you will communicate	• Remember to use chat any time • Now I am going to turn over the floor to the instructor. Let me introduce ______________. Remember to accommodate different learning styles into this—need to script—let them off the hook.

"Hook" & Housekeeping — 1st 15 Minutes of Class

Step	*Time Ref. Cum. Step*	*Topic*	*Objective*	*Instructional Method*	*Screen Design*	*Choreography*	*Production Notes*
1	TBD	Hook	"What's in It for Me?"	To get the participants engaged	Testimonials from various parts of the world	Photos and written subtitles in English with flags from the countries	Audio testimonials in representative languages 10–15 seconds Instructor starts audio and advances the screen in conjunction with the audio We can use a tape recorded script next to the microphone—or we can stream audio—need to verify that plug-ins work
2	—	Welcome	To welcome people to the program and reinforce access to Tech Support access	Lecture	"Welcome to Course" screen	Type phone number in chat room	Ask participants to write down phone number Where is tech support located?
3	—	Facilitator Introductions	To introduce instructor	Lecture	Screen with photo of instructor, short bio, contact information	Instructor introduces him/herself	Give participants 30 seconds to read bio? Should create instructor template page. . . .
4	—	Assistant Facilitator	To introduce the co-instructor and explain his/her role	—	Screen with photo of co-instructor, short bio, contact information	Give asst. microphone in order to introduce himself/herself	Have asst. explain the role Tell participants to send chat to asst. Asst. should be an experienced knowledgeable SME in the content. Answer questions Send questions to instructor Park questions for SME Put checkpoints at end of each module to answer parked chat questions
5	—	Participant Introductions	To introduce participants	Whiteboard	EMEA map	Ask each participant simultaneously to circle where he/she is—write first name on whiteboard	• Then participants should go to the chat to type in full name, location, and job function, and call center experience • Give participants one minute to review map and chat area. • Instructor selects participants with the most interesting experiences and asks them to elaborate. Remember to give speakers the floor; ?? How do we deal with expectations—one thing you would like to get out of the course

							We have already collected some of that info during audio check and instructor should address it when discussing agenda/objectives next, e.g., tell which expectations will or will not be addressed during course.
6	Agenda	To let people know what they are going to experience	Lecture	Bullet points agenda	Instructor elaborates on the agenda and objectives and tells which expectations will or will not be able to be met by the course.	Ask for questions by handraise	Where should breaks be in the agenda? Need to tell participants what they should do if they need to leave their workstations for a short time.
7	Objectives						
8	Pre-Test	N/A	N/A	N/A	N/A	N/A	
9	Environment Tour	Use screen shots of interface with arrows to communication tools	Just remind people about chat and hand raise for now				
10	Ground Rules	To reinforce key ground rules	Lecture	Bullet points	Refer to ground rules handout that was introduced during tech check		
11	Pre-Work/ Prerequisites Review	To acknowledge prework	Lecture				
12	Total 15 minutes for sections	Transition	Say: Now that we've taken care of the preliminaries, let's move on to the next section				

APPENDIX E

Sample Leader Guide

Course Description

Before designing or delivering synchronous courses, it is helpful to understand the learner experience. Learn How to Learn Online focuses on learning in the synchronous environment. It demystifies the technology for the participants so that they have a positive learning experience. The program explores the use of synchronous collaboration tools (whiteboard, chat, audio, and so on), synchronous learning ground rules, and creating the optimal environment for online learning. This session is a prerequisite to all other sessions.

Objectives

At the conclusion of this session, participants will be able to

- Explain a synchronous learning experience
- Explain the role of the learner in the synchronous environment
- Create an effective desktop learning environment for themselves
- Effectively participate in a synchronous learning environment using basic collaboration tools

Target Audience

Anyone new to the synchronous learning experience.

Class Preparation

Prior to Class

- Schedule class
- Send out invitations
- Enroll students (if applicable)
- Distribute participant prework (if applicable)
- Rehearse

Day of Class

- Log on 30 minutes early
- Load appropriate software slides (Placeware, Vclass) as well as LHTLO slides
- Verify URLs are still valid
- Test audio
- Make sure the Introduction slide contains the correct photos and information
- Enable recording

Following Class (If Applicable)

- Send evaluations
- Send follow-up work
- Post discussion questions
- Monitor discussion questions

Description, Timing, Media | *Facilitator Notes* | *Producer Notes*

Getting Ready to Learn Online (Pre-Event Warm-Up)

15 minutes before start of "class"

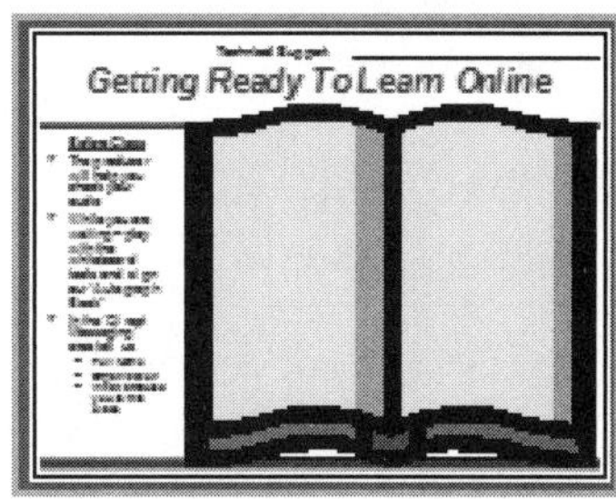

Facilitator Notes:

Write your class start time here: ______________

Make sure you start exactly on time.

Producer Notes:

- Type the technical support phone number on the screen
- Welcome participants by name
- Do audio checks
- Orient to the whiteboard tools

Say: If you're waiting to do an audio check or have already completed yours, please choose a whiteboard tool (such as pen, text, drawing) and sign our autograph book.

Say: Then, in the chat area, tell us your full name (because we can only see your username and sometimes that is different or quirky), where you work, and what attracted you to this class.

Learn How to Learn Online

10 seconds

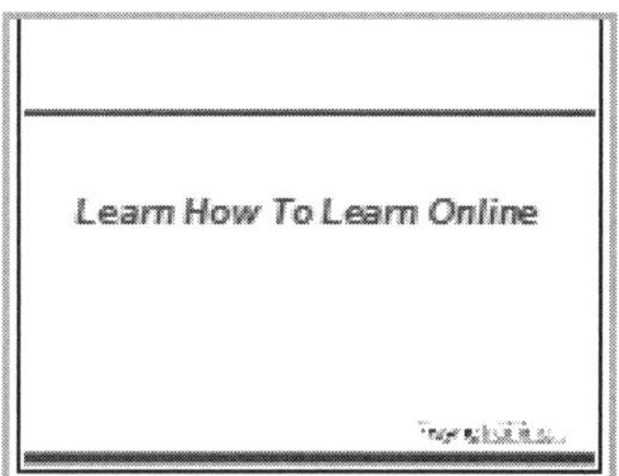

Facilitator Notes:

Make sure you start exactly on time.

Say: Thank you for coming and welcome to Learn How to Learn Online!

We hope at the end of this class you'll have the tools and knowledge you need to become an effective online learner.

Introductions

1 minute

Facilitator Notes:

Say: You all had a chance to introduce yourself in the direct messaging area prior to class.

I hope you took the opportunity to read about your fellow participants.

I am your facilitator: ______________
(Title) ______________
(Experience) ______________.

And I'm here to help you become a successful synchronous learner.

Now, I'd like to introduce you to the producer of today's session.

Producer Notes:

Highlight the email address on screen, as the teaching staff is introduced:

Say: Hi, my name is: ______________
I am here to support you during today's session. Please send me a message in the chat area if you are experiencing technical problems or have logistical questions.

I also will be helping (the facilitator) to manage exercises.

(Continued)

Description, Timing, Media	*Facilitator Notes*	*Producer Notes*

Software-Specific Orientation

10 minutes

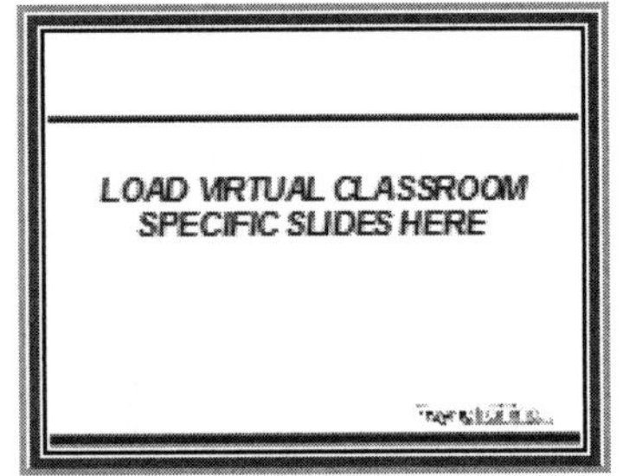

Facilitator Notes:

Explain how to use the basic communication features of the software platform.

Give participants an opportunity to practice.

For example, to teach them how to raise their hands, show the slide that has the raise hand icon, mention where it is located on the screen, and ask them to raise their hands.

Producer Notes:

As features are identified on the whiteboard slides, use the tools to highlight each item.

When possible, use arrows to point out the approximate position on the screen.

Ground Rules

5 minutes

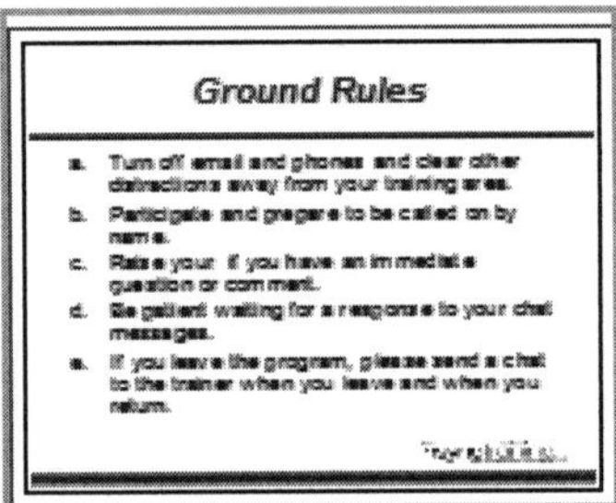

Facilitator Notes:

Call on participants arbitrarily.

Ask them to select a ground rule (no order necessary) and explain why it is important.

Add additional comments as appropriate.

Turn off email and phones and clear other distractions away from your training area. This is important because it is easy to answer the phone or pick up some work and lose track of what is going on in the class. The facilitator will not know that you have "checked out" so he or she won't be able to re-engage you successfully.

Participate and prepare to be called on by name. This is important because the synchronous environment lends itself to interaction. Participation will keep you engaged and move the class along. If participation is low, the facilitator needs to be able to call on people without physical cues.

Raise your hand if you have an immediate question or comment.

When you click the "raise hand" button on your screen, an indicator appears next to your name. This is important because the facilitator cannot tell by looking at you if you are confused on a particular point or have something to add.

Be patient waiting for a response to your chat messages. This is important because the facilitator can't do everything at once. You need to be patient and trust that you will receive a response to your notes.

If you leave the program, please send a chat to the facilitator when you leave and when you return.

This is important because the facilitator needs to know if he or she can call on you—and needs to know that you are not having technical difficulties.

Producer Notes:

Highlight the important words on the ground rule slide.

Use consistent highlights here in order to engage left-brained thinkers (same color, same tool, same highlighting method).

Description, Timing, Media	*Facilitator Notes*	*Producer Notes*

Ground Rules (continued)

Ask Participants:

What other ground rules would you suggest?

Ask participants to answer the following poll question:

Which is the ground rule you will find the most difficult to adhere to today?

Indicate your vote by selecting A, B, C, D, or E.

For Vclass show the A–E polling choices. In other software applications a poll may need to be created.

What Might Keep You from Being a Successful Online Leaner?

1 min to explain

1 min for participants to answer

8 min to debrief

What Might Keep You From Being A Successful Online Learner?

1	2	3	4
5	6	7	8
9	10	11	12

What Might Keep You From Being A Successful Online Learner?

1	2	3	4
5	6	7	8
9	10	11	12
13	14	15	16
17	18	19	20

Ask participates to raise their hands.

Tell participants to note the number next to their hand.

Direct their attention to the grid.

Tell them the box that corresponds to their number is "their box."

Say: you're going to have one minute to answer the question in the whiteboard grid, using the whiteboard tools.

You may use the text tool, pen, picture, or whatever, but be ready to explain it!

Ask: What might keep you from being a successful online learner?

Say: If you have any questions about using the whiteboard tools, please raise your hand.

Say: When you are done, indicate this by checking "yes."

Debrief:

Say: Now let's vote on those items we want to hear more about. Review each block in the grid and put a checkmark in one block that you would like to hear more about.

Pick top five "popular" boxes.

Note: Participants should keep their comments to 30 seconds

Debrief: Call on one participant and ask him or her to explain what he or she meant. If you have helpful comments, make them.
Continue with all remaining participants.

Conclude: So there are a lot of barriers to learning online.
A lot of these issues have to do with learning at your desk.

So now let's explore some ways to make your desktop environment more conducive to learning.

Note: there are two grids in the slide deck. Choose the appropriate slide. If registration is 12 or less, choose the first grid; if 13 to 20, choose the second grid.

After the exercise starts, lower everyone's hands.

Respond to anyone who has raised his or her hand to indicate experiencing trouble with the whiteboard tools.

Keep track of time and give people a 15-second warning.

Clear all the "yeses."

(Continued)

Description, Timing, Media	*Facilitator Notes*	*Producer Notes*
What Ideas Do you Have to Make Your Own Environment More Effective? 5 min What ideas do you have to make your own environment more effective? 1 minute chat exercise	Direct participants to answer the question on the slide by using the chat area. *Say:* list as many ideas as possible! Tell them that they have up to 1 minute to complete this exercise and that they should click "yes" when they are ready. (If appropriate: inform participants to make sure they are sending their messages to "all" participants.) Tell them that if they finish early, they should take the opportunity to review the comments posted by other participants. Call the end of the exercise. Tell participants they have an additional 15 seconds to read the other responses. *Debrief:* Select a few ideas and ask the participant to explain in more detail. Do this with up to five comments. Make additional comments about commonality, differences, good ideas, and so on, if appropriate. *Conclude:* Let's take a look at some very specific ways for you to have a successful learning environment.	Give a 15-second warning. Clear all yeses when participants are done.
The Effective Learning Environment 10 minutes The Effective Learning Environment	*Say:* Ideally, participants should be in private rooms while participating in a synchronous environment. In reality, most participants will learn from their desks. To learn effectively from their desks, participants need to: • Tell co-workers they will be in a class. One way to do this is to send out an email the morning of your class, telling your co-workers when you will be unavailable and why. See your participant guide for a sample email you can send. • Post a sign indicating when class will be over. One facilitator mailed a "Police Line—Do Not Cross" tape to all participants for use during a synchronous class. A participant placed this tape across his office door during the program—and it worked so well, he continued to use it during other periods when he did not want to be disturbed! • Use a headset instead of speakers to minimize workplace disruptions. • Ignore people around them who are signaling for attention. • Turn off the telephone ringer.	Check off points as they are covered.

Description, Timing, Media	*Facilitator Notes*	*Producer Notes*
The Effective Learning Environment (continued)	• Turn off pagers and cell phones. • Turn off email and instant message alerts. • Remove all other tasks and distractions from their desks. Encourage participants to share anecdotes if they have any.	
Role of the Participant in a Synchronous Class 5 minutes 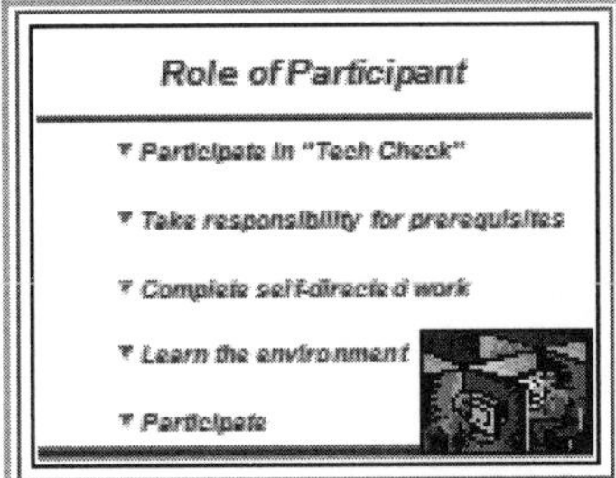 	*Say:* Since kindergarten, or even earlier, we have been learning in pretty much the same way. We go to the teacher's location, we watch and listen to the teacher, and when we leave, we have learned something. (That's the theory, anyway.) We send signals to the teacher by nodding our heads, raising our hands, yawning, and changing our faces to express understanding, confusion, doubt, and a myriad of other emotions. We know how this works, and we understand our role in the process. Now picture a new synchronous participant—let's say it is you. After 20+ years of learning in the traditional manner, you are entering the world of synchronous learning. Let's assume you are willing and able to give this environment a chance. Here is what you have to contend with: • This is a learner-centered environment, which means that you need to take *responsibility* for your own success. • It also means: you don't need to travel to sunny Atlanta (or Akron). You get to stay at your desk and learn from there. And if you are in your office, you will be available to take care of any little emergencies as they come up. • Your live "face-to-face" time will be short—maybe one or two 90-minute sessions. Much of the information that would have been given to you in lecture format is now your responsibility to learn asynchronously. So you need to make sure you read the book, take the tutorial, or watch the video. • You get to stare at a computer screen for two hours at a stretch and hope you can find new ways of sending messages now that you have lost eye contact and body language. • You don't have other participants in proximity with whom to share or commiserate before class, during breaks, and when the facilitator's back is turned.	Annotate screen as appropriate.

(Continued)

Description, Timing, Media	*Facilitator Notes*	*Producer Notes*
Role of the Participant in a Synchronous Class (continued)	So do you have a chance? Will you learn anything? Will those around you take the fact that you are in training seriously? Your experience will have much to do with the tools and training you were given prior to the event. In essence, you need how to learn how to learn all over again. Now we have changed all the rules.	
How Would You Describe Synchronous Learning? 8 minutes 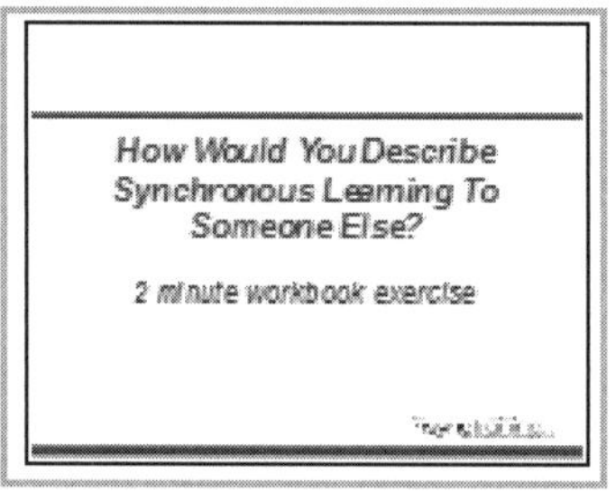 	*Say:* For the past hour or so, you've been participants in a synchronous learning event, many of you for the first time. You probably have an altered perception of what it is, now that you've experienced it. Here's the scenario: You're going to go home tonight and tell your spouse you participated in your first synchronous learning event. And your spouse will say, "HUH?" How would you explain it to him or her? Go to your workbook (page 3) and take 2 minutes to answer this question. Click yes when you are done. Be prepared to share your answer with the class. *Debrief:* After the 2 minutes are over, select a participant at random and ask him or her to read the explanation. Comment yourself and ask for audience input. Repeat with two more participants. *Ask:* Does anyone have anything different to share?	Give 30-second warning. Clear the yeses when the exercise is over. Capture participant's explanation on whiteboard. Include speaker's name. Change font color for each speaker.
AHA! 4 min 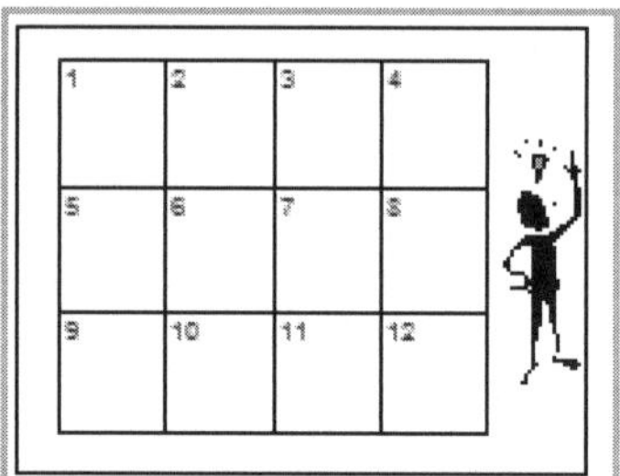 	Ask participates to raise their hands. Tell participants to note the number next to their hands. Direct their attention to the grid. Tell them the box that corresponds to their number is "their box." *Say:* you now have 30 seconds to write one "AHA" you experienced in this session. It can be positive, negative, or emotional. It may relate to the content, the technology, the experience, or your own organization.	*Note:* there are two grids in the slide deck. Choose the appropriate slide. If registration is 12 or less, choose the first grid; if 13 to 20, choose the second grid. After the exercise starts, lower everyone's hands. Clear all the "yeses."

Description, Timing, Media	*Facilitator Notes*	*Producer Notes*

AHA! (continued)

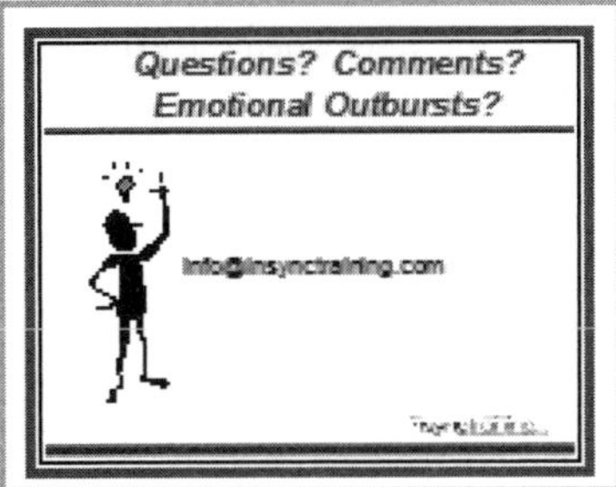

You may use the text tool, pen, picture, or whatever you wish, but be ready to explain it!

Say: When you are done, indicate this by checking "yes."

Wrap Up: Choose three or four "AHas" and make encouraging and supportive comments.

Ask: Does anybody have any questions before we wrap up?

Producer Notes: Write questions and answers on screen.

Conclude: Today you've started on the road to becoming successful online learners. We've explored many of the tools available in most synchronous classrooms (there are more, such as application sharing and break-out rooms) that we didn't demonstrate today.

We certainly hope we will see you online again in future events. You will be receiving an online course evaluation within 2 hours. Please complete that evaluation as soon as possible. We value your feedback.

InSync Center offers a variety of free and fee-based courses that can help you improve your online learning and online training skills.

If you have a question about these or any other programs, please send your questions to info@insynctraining.com.

APPENDIX F

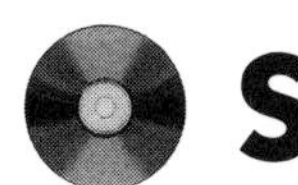

Sample Participant Guide

Welcome to *Learn How to Learn Online*, an online module designed to make you comfortable being a student in cyberspace.

Course Description

Before designing or delivering synchronous courses, you need to make sure you understand the learner experience. Learn How to Learn Online focuses on learning in the synchronous environment. It demystifies the technology for the participants so they have a positive learning experience. The program explores the use of synchronous collaboration tools (whiteboard, chat, audio, and so forth), synchronous learning ground rules, and creating the optimal environment for online learning. This session is a prerequisite to all other sessions.

Objectives

At the conclusion of this session, participants will be able to

- Explain a synchronous learning experience
- Explain the role of the learner in the synchronous environment
- Create an effective desktop learning environment for themselves
- Effectively participate in a synchronous learning environment using basic collaboration tools

Length: 1 hour

Technical Assistance

For technical assistance prior to the event, contact techsupport@insync-training.com. During the class, we will provide you with email and telephone information for live event support.

Prior to the Class

Prior to attending this class, you will receive an email with instructions on how to download and test your virtual classroom software. Please make sure you complete this process at least two business days prior to the event, so that, if you have any difficulty, we have time to assist.

Ground Rules

The online learning environment is new to most of us. If you keep the following ground rules in mind, you will help to create a more effective learning experience for everyone. We will discuss additional ground rules during the online session.

1. Log on to class at least 10 minutes before the scheduled start. This way, class can get started on time.
2. Turn off email and phones and clear other distractions away from your training area. It is easy to answer the phone or pick up some work and lose track of what is going on in the class. The presenter will not know you have "stepped out," so he or she will not be able to re-engage you successfully. Minimizing distractions also improves your computer performance.
3. Participate and prepare to be called on by name. The online learning environment lends itself to interaction. Participation will keep you engaged and move the class along. If participation is low, the presenter must be able to call on people without physical cues.
4. Raise your hand if you have an immediate question or comment. The presenters cannot tell by looking at you if you are confused on a particular point. Asking questions also helps other participants clarify or reinforce concepts.
5. Be patient in waiting for a response to your text message. The presenters are often facilitating the content as well as responding to text chat. Please be patient and trust that you will receive a response to your notes.

Sample Email

This is a sample of a note you can send to co-workers and associates when you are taking an online course.

Dear colleagues,
Today I will be participating in an online class from my desk. I will be online from approximately 1:45 p.m. to 4:00 p.m. I would appreciate it if you would not disturb me during this period of time. If you have an immediate question, please contact Tim Jones at extension 123. If it can wait until after 4:00 p.m., please send me an email and I will follow up with you before the end of the business day.

I appreciate your consideration.

Sincerely,

How would you describe the synchronous learning environment?

APPENDIX G
Resources

Websites

These links are provided for your information only. They do not necessarily reflect an endorsement of the site. Although links are checked from time to time, the link may have changed since our last check.

- ADDIE Model: *www.managersforum.com/astd/2001–2002/ISD-ADDIE.htm*. This website contains a detailed and easy-to-follow explanation for the ADDIE instructional design model.
- ASTD's Roadmap to E-Learning: *www.astd.org/virtual_community/Comm_elrng_rdmap/roadmap.html*. This resource provides guidelines for getting e-learning kick-started in your organization. It includes resources for items like setting up your strategy, preparing your e-learning team, and much more.
- Brandon-hall.com: *www.brandon-hall.com*. Provides objective information and research about using technology for learning.
- Centra's Games Trainers Play Online: *www.centra.com/education/book.asp*. This free downloadable resource provides some creative ways to use many synchronous collaboration tools.
- Distance-Educator.com: *www.distance-educator.com*. Provides information and access to expertise on distance teaching and learning.
- Instant Co-Browsing: Lightweight Real-Time Collaborative Web Browsing: *http://www2002.org/CDROM/poster/86/*. This paper, out of Mitsubshi Electric Research Laboratories, provides information on a

collaborative web-browsing system created by that organization. It is useful because it explains the concept of collaborative web browsing in detail.

- InSync Training: *www.insynctraining.com*. Tips, techniques, and resources for synchronous learning. Entryway for "InSync Center," a free online community for synchronous training professionals. This community provides its users with access to virtual classrooms, meeting rooms, discussion boards, and a variety of other collaboration tools.
- Learning Circuits and Learning Circuits Archive: *www.learningcircuits.org*. ASTD's online magazine all about eLearning.
- Masie Center: *www.masie.com*. The Masie Center is an international think tank located in Saratoga Springs, New York. The Center is dedicated to exploring the intersection of learning and technology.
- Online collaboration resource: *www.cvm.tamu.edu/wklemm/cl2.html*. This short page provides a definition of the value of computer conferencing for collaborative learning.
- The Studio of Saul Carliner: *http://saulcarliner.home.att.net/*. Content development for the workplace.

Books

2000/2001 ASTD Distance Learning Yearbook: The Newest Trends and Technologies by Karen Mantyla (ASTD, 2001).

This handy one-volume resource includes information on creating distance learning proposals and pilot programs; Internet-based training, videoconferencing, and other technologies; setting up and administering a program; career development for trainers; and more.

The AMA Handbook of E-Learning: Effective Design, Implementation, and Technology Solutions by George Piskurich (Ed.) (American Management Association, 2003).

This authoritative sourcebook is a timely decision-making tool for companies making the transition to (or already using) e-learning. Featuring all-original contributions from high-profile practitioners and renowned theorists, the book reveals how top companies are implementing and using this crucial employee development tool.

Collaboration Handbook by M. Winer and K. Ray. (Amherst Wilder Foundation, 1994).

This book explains how to achieve collaboration, what problems to anticipate, and how to maximize the results of your collaboration.

The Synchronous Trainer's Survival Guide: Facilitating Successful Live and Online Courses, Meetings, and Events by Jennifer Hofmann (Pfeiffer, 2003).

A hands-on resource for enhancing your real-time e-learning sessions. It is the first book focusing solely on this emerging training method. If you're new to synchronous training, everything you need to know is right here. If you're a seasoned pro, the practical tips, tools, and customizable templates in this book will ensure the success of your online training courses, meetings, and events.

Web-Based Training: Using Technology to Design Adult Learning Experiences (2nd ed.) by Margaret Driscoll (Pfeiffer, 2002).

This book is written for instructional designers, adult educators, training and human resource managers, and workplace educators developing their first web-based training program.

Articles

Driscoll, M., & Rocky, C. (2002, September) Teaching technical skills & knowledge in the live virtual classroom: 20 best practices for using application sharing. *ASTD Newsletter.*

Kontzer, T. (2003, June 5). Collaboration hard to define, even for experts. *Information Week.* Available: www.informationweek.com/story/showArticle.jhtml?articleID=10300343

This article summarizes the opinions of experts regarding what collaboration really means.

Schlessman-Frost, A. (1994, December). Collaboration in adult ESL and family literacy education. *ERIC Digest.* Available: www.cal.org/ncle/digests/SCHLESSM.HTM

This resource discusses the impact of collaboration specifically in regard to family literacy issues.

APPENDIX H
Glossary

Awareness of the following web-based learning terms will assist you as you create effective synchronous programs:

ADDIE System of Instructional Design. ADDIE is an instructional design technique methodology: individual steps are to Assess and analyze needs, Design instruction and presentations, Develop materials, Implement activities and courses, and Evaluate participant progress and instructional materials effectiveness.

Annotation. An annotation is a drawing or text comment placed on the whiteboard during a synchronous event by the trainer or participant using whiteboard drawing tools.

Application Viewing/Sharing. A feature that allows the facilitator to share applications with participants. For example, a facilitator may use application sharing to have participants alter a Microsoft Excel document, even though the participants do not have Excel installed on their own computers.

Asynchronous Learning. "Asynchronous" refers to instruction that is not constrained by geography or time. Everyone involved in an asynchronous activity performs his or her part on his or her own time.

Audio. The most common synchronous medium. Using audio, the facilitator and participants can talk to one another over the Internet or through a phone bridge (teleconferencing). One-way audio (only the facilitator can speak) or two-way audio (both the facilitator and participants can speak) is available in most synchronous software packages.

Auditory Learners. Auditory learners learn most effectively when they hear the information.

Bandwidth. The speed at which information is transferred via modem or other network-access device to Internet users. The greater the bandwidth, the more quickly the data (audio, video, text) reaches the user.

Blended Learning. A combination—or blend—of different learning technologies. Blended learning is becoming increasingly common with the availability of both synchronous and asynchronous web-learning options. An example is a course that consists of an asynchronous web module that covers content and a follow-up synchronous module that allows participants to apply the content.

Breakout Sessions. A feature available in some synchronous software packages that allows the facilitator to break a class into smaller groups. Participants are able to interact within their smaller groups and rejoin the main classroom to share their findings with the whole group.

Chat. A real-time text conversation between users over the Internet. Whatever a user types is displayed on the other users' screens as it is entered. Some synchronous software packages offer a chat function; it provides an avenue for interaction between participants and trainer. Chat dialogues can often be saved for later reference.

Computer-Assisted Instruction. A term used commonly in education to describe instruction in which a computer is used as a learning tool.

Computer-Based Learning. An all-encompassing term used to describe any computer-delivered learning, including CD-ROM and the World Wide Web.

Desktop Learning. Any learning delivered by computer at the participant's desk.

Desktop Video Conferencing. A real-time conference using live pictures between two or more people who communicate via computer on a network.

Discussion Board. An asynchronous feature that allows participants to post messages and reply to messages by topic. Discussion boards are different from chat in that they are not real-time.

eLearning. A term used to describe electronically delivered learning methods delivered on media such as CD-ROM or the Internet. They may include online assessments, web-based reinforcement tools, and online coaching.

Evaluation. A test-like feature that enables a trainer to conduct pre- and post-session assessments and to monitor participants' understanding of course material as it is being presented. Assessment results can be automatically tabulated and saved.

Extranet. A website for existing customers rather than the general public. It can provide access to paid research, current inventories, internal databases, and virtually any other information that is published for a limited audience. An extranet uses the public Internet as its transmission system but requires passwords to gain access.

Firewall. A set of software programs that keeps a network secure. Firewalls are widely used to give users access to the Internet in a secure fashion as well as to separate a company's public web server from its internal network. They are also used to keep internal network segments secure—for example, a research or accounting subnet that might be vulnerable to snooping from within.

Google. A popular Internet search engine that allows users to search the World Wide Web using key words. http://www.google.com

Hyperlinks. An element in an electronic document that can link to another place either within the same document or in a different document. Typically the user clicks the hyperlink to follow the link.

Hypertext Markup Language (HTML). The authoring language used to create documents that can be viewed via the World Wide Web.

Instant Messaging. The ability to conduct a one-on-one text-based discussion over the Internet.

Instructional Design/Instructional Systems Design (ISD). ISD is the entire process of analysis of learning needs and goals and the development of a delivery system to meet those needs.

Internet-Based Training. Training that can be conducted over the Internet. Usually this is done with the World Wide Web, but email correspondence courses and file transfers also fall into this category.

Internet Service Provider (ISP). An organization that provides access to the Internet. Examples include America Online® and Earthlink®. For a fee, a website can be created and maintained on the ISP's server, allowing a smaller organization to have a presence on the web with its own domain name.

Intranet. An in-house website that serves the employees of an organization. Although intranet pages may link to the Internet, an intranet is not a site accessed by the general public. Intranets use the same communications protocols and hypertext links as the web and thus provide a standard way of distributing information internally and extending the application worldwide at the same time.

Intranet-Based Training. Training provided through a company's internal network. Web browsers are used to access company pages. The primary characteristic is that content is accessible only within the company's internal network.

Kinesthetic Learners. Kinesthetic learners require physical movement and action in order to learn effectively.

Learning Management System (LMS). Software that automates the administration of training events. All learning management systems manage the log-in of registered users, manage course catalogs, record data from learners, and provide reports to management.

Learning Technologies. Any tool or technology that facilitates learning. This includes classroom, correspondence, books, audiotapes, teleconferencing, interactive television, CD-ROM, and the World Wide Web.

Needs Analysis. Formal process of identifying discrepancies between a learner's current performance and the desired performance.

Online Collaboration. People working together, using asynchronous and synchronous online tools, should be able to obtain results (solve problems, create project plans, design projects, and so forth) that are better than the results they would have found by working independently.

Online Learning. An all-encompassing term that refers to any learning done with a computer over a network, including a company's intranet, the company's local area network (LAN), and the Internet.

Pacing/Comprehension. A feature in synchronous software programs that allows participants to continually apprise the trainer on the pace and clarity of the delivery.

Plug-In. Software typically downloaded from the web that enables the user to read, hear, or view something. Examples of plug-ins include Adobe Acrobat® Reader to view documents, RealPlayer® audio to listen to sound or music, and Flash™ to view animation and graphics and listen to audio.

Portal. A web "supersite" that provides a variety of services, including web searching, news, white and yellow pages directories, free email, discussion groups, online shopping, and links to other sites. Web portals are the web equivalent of original online services such as CompuServe® and AOL. Although the term was initially used to refer to general-purpose sites, it is increasingly being used to refer to market sites that offer the same services, but only to a particular industry, such as banking, insurance, or computers.

Producer. A person who assists the trainer during live synchronous events by acting as an "extra set of hands." In addition to training responsibilities, the producer handles technical support so that the trainer can focus on instruction. The producer does not need to be in the same physical location as the trainer.

Record/Playback. Feature that allows the trainer and participant to record synchronous events, play them back later, and edit them into asynchronous sessions. This feature benefits individuals who miss sessions and allows quick creation of asynchronous learning content.

Self-Paced Learning. Learning that is taken at a time, pace, and place that are chosen by the participant. Generally, there is no interaction (synchronous or asynchronous) with a trainer.

Survey/Poll. A quick way to check the pulse of the class. Questions can be true-false, multiple-choice, or other formats.

Synchronous Learning. This term refers to instruction that is led by a trainer in real time. Examples of synchronous interactions include traditional trainer-led classrooms, conference calls, instant messages, videoconferences, whiteboard sessions, and synchronous online classrooms/classroom software.

Synchronous Web Browsing. Element that allows trainers or participants to bring the class to a specific Internet or intranet site. A variation of the feature allows the use of browsers to run short, self-paced exercises on the Internet or intranet as part of a synchronous session.

Visual Learners. Visual learners predominantly rely on their sense of sight to take in new data, understand it, and remember it. They need to be able to "see" something to fully understand it.

VoIP. Technically, this is "Voice delivered over the Internet Protocol." This means sending voice information in digital form using the Internet.

Web Streaming. Live playback of audio or video files on the web. Usually involves a plug-in or applications program to execute the media file.

Whiteboard. An application used in synchronous interactive web conferencing that allows documents and content materials to be posted on the screen for all participants to see. The participants see the information being changed on their screens in real time. Whiteboards work well for visual symbols, charts, and graphs.

About the Author

Jennifer Hofmann has a master's degree in instructional technology and distance education and a bachelor's degree in business and finance. Jennifer is the principal eLearning consultant and owner of InSync Training, LLC, a consulting firm that specializes in the design and delivery of synchronous and blended eLearning. Her team provides workshops and development services to individuals and organizations that wish to implement a synchronous classroom. She is the moderator of InSync Center, a web community dedicated to sharing the best practices of synchronous training professionals. In the field since 1997, she has experience using all of the major synchronous delivery platforms.

Jennifer is the author of *The Synchronous Trainer's Survival Guide* (Pfeiffer, 2003). She is also a contributor to the American Management Association's *Handbook of eLearning*. Jennifer has made many contributions to *Learning Circuits*, the ASTD online webzine dedicated to eLearning topics (www.learningcircuits.org). She is a regular speaker on synchronous and blended eLearning at national industry events and has taught the Certified Online Instructor Program at the Walden Institute. Contact Jennifer by sending an email message to jennifer@insynctraining.com.

About InSync

InSync Training, LLC, is the industry leader in the design, development, and delivery of synchronous training and education. Owned by Jennifer Hofmann, author of The *Synchronous Trainer's Survival Guide*, InSync offers a variety of consulting, development, and delivery services to support synchronous training initiatives. Some of the services provided include:

- Expertise in synchronous training platforms;
- Experienced project management and design team;
- Synchronous facilitation services; and
- Synchronous training workshops, including train-the-trainer live event production services.

InSync is on the Web at www.insynctraining.com or contact Jennifer directly at Jennifer@insynctraining.com.

Feedback

Any feedback, tips, or techniques you can provide will be considered for future publications.

☐ Suggestions for Improvement

☐ Examples and Anecdotes

☐ Tips and Techniques

☐ Useful Resources

☐ Sample Checklists or Job Aids

Please email your feedback directly to the author at Jennifer@ insynctraining.com.

How to Use the CD-ROM

System Requirements

Windows PC

- 486 or Pentium processor-based personal computer
- Microsoft Windows 95 or Windows NT 3.51 or later
- Minimum RAM: 8MB for Windows 95 and NT
- Available space on hard disk: 8 MB Windows 95 and NT
- 2X speed CD-ROM drive or faster

Macintosh

- Macintosh with a 68020 or higher processor or Power Macintosh
- Apple OS version 7.0 or later
- Minimum RAM: 12MB for Macintosh
- Available space on hard disk: 6MB Macintosh
- 2X speed CD-ROM drive or faster

NOTE: This CD-ROM requires Netscape 3.0 or MS Internet Explorer 3.0 or higher. You can download these products using the links on the CD-ROM Help Page.

Getting Started

Insert the CD-ROM into your drive. The CD-ROM will usually launch automatically. If it does not, click on the CD-ROM drive on your computer to launch. After you click to agree to the terms of the Copyright Page, the Home Page will appear.

Moving Around

Use the buttons at the left of each screen to move among the menu pages. To view a document listed on one of the menu pages, simply click on the name of the document. To quit a document at any time, click the box at the upper right-hand corner of the screen.

To quit the CD-ROM, you can click the Exit button or hit Alt-F4.

To Download Documents

Open the document you wish to download. Under the File pulldown menu, choose Save As. Save the document onto your hard drive with a different name. It is important to use a different name, otherwise the document may remain a read-only file.

You can also click on your CD drive in Windows Explorer and select a document to copy it to your hard drive and rename it.

In Case of Trouble

If you experience difficulty using this CD-ROM, please follow these steps:

1. Make sure your hardware and systems configurations conform to the systems requirements noted under "Systems Requirements" above.
2. Review the installation procedure for your type of hardware and operating system. It is possible to reinstall the software if necessary.
3. Have a question, comment, or suggestion? Contact us! We value your feedback, and we want to hear from you.

For questions about this or other Pfeiffer products, you may contact us by:

E-mail: customer@wiley.com
Mail: Customer Care Wiley/Pfeiffer
10475 Crosspoint Blvd.
Indianapolis, IN 46256
Phone: (U.S.) 800-274-4434 (Outside the U.S. 317-572-3985)
Fax: (U.S.) 800-569-0443 (Outside the U.S. 317-572-4002)

To order additional copies of this product or to browse other Pfeiffer products visit us online at www.pfeiffer.com.

To speak with someone in Product Technical Support, call 800-762-2974 or 317-572-3994 Monday through Friday 8:30 a.m. to 5 p.m. (EST). You can also contact Product Technical Support and get support information through our website at http://www.wiley.com/techsupport

Before calling or writing, please have the following information available:

- Type of operating system
- Any error messages displayed
- Complete description of the problem

It is best if you are sitting at your computer when making the call.

Pfeiffer Publications Guide

This guide is designed to familiarize you with the various types of Pfeiffer publications. The formats section describes the various types of products that we publish; the methodologies section describes the many different ways that content might be provided within a product. We also provide a list of the topic areas in which we publish.

FORMATS

In addition to its extensive book-publishing program, Pfeiffer offers content in an array of formats, from fieldbooks for the practitioner to complete, ready-to-use training packages that support group learning.

FIELDBOOK Designed to provide information and guidance to practitioners in the midst of action. Most fieldbooks are companions to another, sometimes earlier, work, from which its ideas are derived; the fieldbook makes practical what was theoretical in the original text. Fieldbooks can certainly be read from cover to cover. More likely, though, you'll find yourself bouncing around following a particular theme, or dipping in as the mood, and the situation, dictate.

HANDBOOK A contributed volume of work on a single topic, comprising an eclectic mix of ideas, case studies, and best practices sourced by practitioners and experts in the field.

An editor or team of editors usually is appointed to seek out contributors and to evaluate content for relevance to the topic. Think of a handbook not as a ready-to-eat meal, but as a cookbook of ingredients that enables you to create the most fitting experience for the occasion.

RESOURCE Materials designed to support group learning. They come in many forms: a complete, ready-to-use exercise (such as a game); a comprehensive resource on one topic (such as conflict management) containing a variety of methods and approaches; or a collection of like-minded activities (such as icebreakers) on multiple subjects and situations.

TRAINING PACKAGE An entire, ready-to-use learning program that focuses on a particular topic or skill. All packages comprise a guide for the facilitator/trainer and a workbook for the participants. Some packages are supported with additional media—such as video—or learning aids, instruments, or other devices to help participants understand concepts or practice and develop skills.

- *Facilitator/trainer's guide* Contains an introduction to the program, advice on how to organize and facilitate the learning event, and step-by-step instructor notes. The guide also contains copies of presentation materials—handouts, presentations, and overhead designs, for example—used in the program.
- *Participant's workbook* Contains exercises and reading materials that support the learning goal and serves as a valuable reference and support guide for participants in the weeks and months that follow the learning event. Typically, each participant will require his or her own workbook.

ELECTRONIC CD-ROMs and web-based products transform static Pfeiffer content into dynamic, interactive experiences. Designed to take advantage of the searchability, automation, and ease-of-use that technology provides, our e-products bring convenience and immediate accessibility to your workspace.

METHODOLOGIES

CASE STUDY A presentation, in narrative form, of an actual event that has occurred inside an organization. Case studies are not prescriptive, nor are they used to prove a point; they are designed to develop critical analysis and decision-making skills. A case study has a specific time frame, specifies a sequence of events, is narrative in structure, and contains a plot structure—an issue (what should be/have been done?). Use case studies when the goal is to enable participants to apply previously learned theories to the circumstances in the case, decide what is pertinent, identify the real issues, decide what should have been done, and develop a plan of action.

ENERGIZER A short activity that develops readiness for the next session or learning event. Energizers are most commonly used after a break or lunch to stimulate or refocus the group. Many involve some form of physical activity, so they are a useful way to counter post-lunch lethargy. Other uses include transitioning from one topic to another, where "mental" distancing is important.

EXPERIENTIAL LEARNING ACTIVITY (ELA) A facilitator-led intervention that moves participants through the learning cycle from experience to application (also known as a Structured Experience). ELAs are carefully thought-out designs in which there is a definite learning purpose and intended outcome. Each step—everything that participants do during the activity—facilitates the accomplishment of the stated goal. Each ELA includes complete instructions for facilitating the intervention and a clear statement of goals, suggested group size and timing, materials required, an explanation of the process, and, where appropriate, possible variations to the activity. (For more detail on Experiential Learning Activities, see the Introduction to the *Reference Guide to Handbooks and Annuals*, 1999 edition, Pfeiffer, San Francisco.)

GAME A group activity that has the purpose of fostering team sprit and togetherness in addition to the achievement of a pre-stated goal. Usually contrived—undertaking a desert expedition, for example—this type of learning method offers an engaging means for participants to demonstrate and practice business and interpersonal skills. Games are effective for team building and personal development mainly because the goal is subordinate to the process—the means through which participants reach decisions, collaborate, communicate, and generate trust and understanding. Games often engage teams in "friendly" competition.

ICEBREAKER A (usually) short activity designed to help participants overcome initial anxiety in a training session and/or to acquaint the participants with one another. An icebreaker can be a fun activity or can be tied to specific topics or training goals. While a useful tool in itself, the icebreaker comes into its own in situations where tension or resistance exists within a group.

INSTRUMENT A device used to assess, appraise, evaluate, describe, classify, and summarize various aspects of human behavior. The term used to describe an instrument depends primarily on its format and purpose. These terms include survey, questionnaire, inventory, diagnostic, survey, and poll. Some uses of instruments include providing instrumental feedback to group members, studying here-and-now processes or functioning within a group, manipulating group composition, and evaluating outcomes of training and other interventions.

Instruments are popular in the training and HR field because, in general, more growth can occur if an individual is provided with a method for focusing specifically on his or her own behavior. Instruments also are used to obtain information that will serve as a basis for change and to assist in workforce planning efforts.

Paper-and-pencil tests still dominate the instrument landscape with a typical package comprising a facilitator's guide, which offers advice on administering the instrument and interpreting the collected data, and an initial set of instruments. Additional instruments are available separately. Pfeiffer, though, is investing heavily in e-instruments. Electronic instrumentation provides effortless distribution and, for larger groups particularly, offers advantages over paper-and-pencil tests in the time it takes to analyze data and provide feedback.

LECTURETTE A short talk that provides an explanation of a principle, model, or process that is pertinent to the participants' current learning needs. A lecturette is intended to establish a common language bond between the trainer and the participants by providing a mutual frame of reference. Use a lecturette as an introduction to a group activity or event, as an interjection during an event, or as a handout.

MODEL A graphic depiction of a system or process and the relationship among its elements. Models provide a frame of reference and something more tangible, and more easily remembered, than a verbal explanation. They also give participants something to "go on," enabling them to track their own progress as they experience the dynamics, processes, and relationships being depicted in the model.

ROLE PLAY A technique in which people assume a role in a situation/scenario: a customer service rep in an angry-customer exchange, for example. The way in which the role is approached is then discussed and feedback is offered. The role play is often repeated using a different approach and/or incorporating changes made based on feedback received. In other words, role playing is a spontaneous interaction involving realistic behavior under artificial (and safe) conditions.

SIMULATION A methodology for understanding the interrelationships among components of a system or process. Simulations differ from games in that they test or use a model that depicts or mirrors some aspect of reality in form, if not necessarily in content. Learning occurs by studying the effects of change on one or more factors of the model. Simulations are commonly used to test hypotheses about what happens in a system—often referred to as "what if?" analysis—or to examine best-case/worst-case scenarios.

THEORY A presentation of an idea from a conjectural perspective. Theories are useful because they encourage us to examine behavior and phenomena through a different lens.

TOPICS

The twin goals of providing effective and practical solutions for workforce training and organization development and meeting the educational needs of training and human resource professionals shape Pfeiffer's publishing program. Core topics include the following:

Leadership & Management
Communication & Presentation
Coaching & Mentoring
Training & Development
E-Learning
Teams & Collaboration
OD & Strategic Planning
Human Resources
Consulting

Customer Care

Have a question, comment, or suggestion? Contact us! We value your feedback and we want to hear from you.

For questions about this or other Pfeiffer products, you may contact us by:

E-mail: **customer@wiley.com**

Mail: **Customer Care Wiley/Pfeiffer**
10475 Crosspoint Blvd.
Indianapolis, IN 46256

Phone: **(US) 800-274-4434** (Outside the US: 317-572-3985)

Fax: **(US) 800-569-0443** (Outside the US: 317-572-4002)

To order additional copies of this title or to browse other Pfeiffer products, visit us online at **www.pfeiffer.com**.

For **Technical Support** questions call **(800) 274-4434.**

For authors guidelines, log on to www.pfeiffer.com and click on "Resources for Authors."

If you are . . .

A **college bookstore, a professor, an instructor, or work in higher education** and you'd like to place an order or request an exam copy, please contact jbreview@wiley.com.

A **general retail bookseller** and you'd like to establish an account or speak to a local sales representative, contact Melissa Grecco at 201-748-6267 or mgrecco@wiley.com.

An **exclusively on-line bookseller**, contact Amy Blanchard at 530-756-9456 or ablanchard@wiley.com or Jennifer Johnson at 206-568-3883 or jjohnson@wiley.com, both of our Online Sales department.

A **librarian or library representative**, contact John Chambers in our Library Sales department at 201-748-6291 or jchamber@wiley.com.

A **reseller, training company/consultant, or corporate trainer**, contact Charles Regan in our Special Sales department at 201-748-6553 or cregan@wiley.com.

A **specialty retail distributor** (includes specialty gift stores, museum shops, and corporate bulk sales), contact Kim Hendrickson in our Special Sales department at 201-748-6037 or khendric@wiley.com.

Purchasing for the **Federal government**, contact Ron Cunningham in our Special Sales department at 317-572-3053 or rcunning@wiley.com.

Purchasing for a **State or Local government**, contact Charles Regan in our Special Sales department at 201-748-6553 or cregan@wiley.com.